To Ella
Xmas 1909
fr

D1381302

A
THOUGHT
FOR
EACH DAY
IN
1970

The Friendship Book

OF

FRANCIS GAY

·

1970

D. C. THOMSON & CO. LTD.
London   Glasgow   Manchester   Dundee

What is the worth of anything,
But for the happiness 'twill bring?

RICHARD OWEN CAMBRIDGE

EYES FRONT!

Whatever your goal in life you'll find
You never will reach it by looking behind,
By turning to see what other folks do,
Or fearing some chap's running better than you.

DAVID HOPE

A

LOVELY WORLD

Oh Jill, I love your little ways,
Your eager questing eyes,
The joy you find in everything ;
So new, yet wise.

DAVID HOPE

JANUARY

I CAN see it now. I can even smell the ink in that exercise book I used as a boy of eight.

That's a long, long time ago, but how vividly I recall the master handing out those new books. I was in a new class. It was the beginning of a new year. We also had new pens, even a new square of blotting-paper. All of us did our sums so carefully—no blots, no smudges, and the date underlined.

My own work was much the same on the second day of term. On the third, I made a blot, tried to rub it out and finished up with an ugly smudge. I had hoped to fill the book with sums, all of them perfect and ticked in red. But it didn't work out like that. It became less and less tidy as time went on till the teacher wrote, " Disgraceful," before the book was even half full.

A bit like life ? Some folk say there's no point in a fresh beginning when a year is new. But I feel that the early days of 1970 give us a splendid chance to do a bit better in the coming weeks than we did in 1969. At any rate, there's no harm in trying !

THESE few words were once spoken by Abraham Lincoln :

" I am not bound to win, but I am bound to be true. I am not bound to succeed, but I am bound to live up to what light I have. I must stand with anybody that stands right ; stand with him while he *is* right, and part with him when he goes wrong."

They're worth thinking about.

SATURDAY—JANUARY 3.

I THINK this is probably an old traditional tale. Nevertheless, I am sure it has just as much meaning now as it ever did.

It seems that a man managed to find a way to exert power over the spirits, and was told that he would be granted three wishes.

Immediately, the man wished for money and it was granted to him. So he began to live the life of the rich, and soon he became an alcoholic.

To recover his former health the man had to use his second wish, leaving him with only one more. Undecided and confused, he ended up by using his third wish to restore himself completely to his former state and have the whole incident erased from his memory.

I have no more power over the spirits than you do. But this story is still food for thought.

SUNDAY—JANUARY 4.

IF God be for us, who can be against us?

MONDAY—JANUARY 5.

FUNNY thing is memory,
A conjuror, I'd say,
Or so it seems as I look back
To things of yesterday.
For half the sorrows are forgot,
And I remember best
The sunshine lighting up my road,
The times when I've been blessed.
The ill is lost, the good remains,
The worst is left behind ;
And all life's precious little joys
Have nested in my mind !

THE FRIENDSHIP BOOK

TUESDAY—JANUARY 6.

IN an attempt to get some help in raising money for a local cause, the Lady of the House called on one of her acquaintances, saying, " We should be so glad to see you on the day, and so grateful for a couple of hours' help with the teas."

But she failed in her mission. The lady concerned said she was terribly sorry, but she just hadn't the time.

Well, that being so, there was no more to say—except the not unkindly remark my wife made after the effort was over : " You know, dear, I'm rather sorry I didn't persuade her to join us. She has less to do than anybody else I know. She would have enjoyed it enormously. Queer, isn't it, how people with most time on their hands are least able to help with a good cause?"

WEDNESDAY—JANUARY 7.

IT'S not much fun, day scarce begun,
*   To leave your cosy bed ;*
And turning out, with snow about . . .
*   The path of work to tread,*
But has the thought occurred to you,
*   Some folk CAN'T do what you can do?*

THURSDAY—JANUARY 8.

IF things keep going wrong and you're getting fed-up, think about this quotation by Jacob Riis.

" When nothing seems to help, I go and look at a stone-cutter hammering away at a rock, perhaps 100 times, without so much as a crack showing in it.

" Yet at the 101st blow it will split in two, and I know it was not that last blow that did it, but all that had gone before."

FRIDAY—JANUARY 9.

THE civic authorities of Hamilton in Canada once ordered a tree to be cut down.

One of the woodcutters climbed up among the branches, and discovered a nest with three eggs in it. "We can't cut the tree down yet," he said—and after some debate the authorities agreed to allow it to remain till the eggs were hatched and the young birds away from the nest.

A month or two later the tree was felled. The men who did the job were fascinated by the way in which the nest had been made. Bit by bit they pulled the grass, twigs and moss apart, and found the bird had also used hundreds of tiny scraps of paper, tightly rolled.

When the men looked more closely, they saw that many of the scraps of paper were from a Bible—and on one were the words—"*Trust in the Lord.*"

SATURDAY—JANUARY 10.

IT is many, many years since a friend in the U.S.A. sent me this summary of practical wisdom, but I still remember it. Perhaps you would like to think it over?

The world would be better off if people tried to become better, and people would become better if they stopped trying to be better off. For when everybody tries to become better off, nobody is better off; but when everybody tries to become better, everybody is better off.

SUNDAY—JANUARY 11.

WALK while ye have the light, lest darkness come upon you.

THE FRIENDSHIP BOOK

ALL his days, George Gibb, of Paisley, has made a point of looking for the best in everything. At a time when he and his wife, Jean, were celebrating fifty happy years together, enclosed with his letter to me were these lines, in which I believe he sums up the secret of his life :

Do you wish for kindness ? Be kind.
Do you wish for truth ? Be true.
What you give of yourself, you find,
Your world's a reflection of you.
It's in loving, not being loved,
The heart is most truly blessed,
It's in giving, not seeking gifts,
That we gain what is brightest and best.

LAST week a neighbour of mine did his good deed. Some months ago he knocked down his old wooden fence, pulled up the posts, bit by bit, chopped up the pieces, stored them in an orderly manner (he likes everything just so), and boasted in his gentle, humorous way that he had enough dry wood to light all the fires he would ever sit by.

A good-sized bundle of that wood went last week into Mrs William Morrison's shed, and she thanked my neighbour for it. She said she was very grateful—she'd been running short of kindling. And she also said she had some fine, sound cooking apples, and my neighbour was to take them home to his wife. He said, " Not on your life."

She said, " Your arms'll ache carrying the wood back."

Then they looked at each other, and smiled.

I like people who are independent in spirit.

WEDNESDAY—JANUARY 14.

F OR most of us life's pretty grim
And yet I somehow find
Good folk around, brave folk abound,
And lots of folk are kind.
So much there is to make us sad,
But, oh, so much to make us glad.

THURSDAY—JANUARY 15.

MRS HELEN BLACK is well past seventy, and any morning of the week, be it sun, rain, sleet or snow, you'll see her out on her message round.

She'll be paying the papers for one neighbour, collecting groceries for another, or popping into the post office for someone else. All this, mind you, though she can't walk without the help of two sticks.

It doesn't just stop there, either. One morning the other week, an old body in her eighties answered a knock at the door and found Helen on the step. Can you guess why she'd come? To do the spring cleaning! She knew her old friend hadn't been too well, and that spring-cleaning the house would be too much for her.

In a twinkling, Helen was into her apron and to work. She scrubbed and polished, beat the rugs, and dusted the house from top to bottom. When she'd finished, it was neat as a new pin, and the gratitude shining in the eyes of her friend was all the reward she wanted.

How does Helen manage it? Because she doesn't waste time looking wistfully back to days gone by, but steps bravely forward towards tomorrow. That, surely, is how to make the most of the best, and the best of the worst!

FRIDAY—JANUARY 16.

A SIMPLETON went into a bank,
And said with the greatest of ease :
" I'd like to draw out fifty pounds
In ten-shilling notes, if you please."
The cashier replied, " Ah, well, well,
You must pardon me, sir, if I grin ;
But you cannot take anything out,
For you haven't put anything in !"
The moral is easy to see—
You have seen it already, no doubt—
If you put little into each day
I'm afraid you won't get a lot out !

SATURDAY—JANUARY 17.

AS a young woman, Margaret Ellis was an army nurse in the First World War. In field hospitals she came face to face with the horror of war, and it left its mark on her. So much so, I am told, that after the war when she went home to Scotland, she decided to devote her life to caring for new-born babies. For years she had grieved at the death of many a soldier she had tended. Now, instead, she would rejoice at life that was just beginning.

So it was for nearly fifty years. And when she died at seventy-eight, many of " her " children returned to pay their last tribute to her. Together, they crowded into the kirk at Ladybank, the titled and wealthy side by side with ordinary folk.

Fittingly, the service ended not with a hymn of sorrow, but one of happiness, echoing the songs of the bairns who meant so much to her:

Children of the Heavenly King,
As ye journey, sweetly sing ;
Sing your Saviour's worthy praise,
Glorious in His works and ways . . .

SUNDAY—JANUARY 18.

YEA, though I walk through the valley of the shadow of death, I will fear no evil: for Thou art with me; Thy rod and staff they comfort me.

MONDAY—JANUARY 19.

ONCE upon a time Aesop was sitting by the road when a traveller stopped and asked him, "What sort of people live in Athens?"

"Tell me where you come from," replied Aesop.

"Oh," said the traveller, frowning, "I come from Argos—a wretched place, full of liars and thieves and unfriendly people."

Said Aesop sadly, "I'm sorry to tell you, friend, you'll find the people of Athens just the same!"

Presently another traveller came by, and he, too, asked what sort of people lived in Athens, to which Aesop again said, "Tell me where you come from."

"Oh," said the traveller, smiling, "I come from the kindest city in the world—Argos, where everyone was decent and easy to get on with . . ."

Said Aesop, "Friend, I'm glad to say that you'll find the people of Athens just the same!"

TUESDAY—JANUARY 20.

I'M no mathematician, and maybe you aren't, either. But I don't think we need to be to work out this sum. It was sent to me by Mr James Allan, of London.

He asks: If you were paid a shilling for each kind and helpful word you spoke, and fined sixpence for every hurtful word you said, would you be richer or poorer at the end of the day?

It's simple enough—but how much depends on the answer!

THE FRIENDSHIP BOOK

THE things you see on your TV
Sure make you wonder if
The whole world's bad as well as mad—
Maybe it scares you stiff.
But what you rarely get is news
To warm your heart each day:
The gentle, loving things folk do,
The kindly things they say.
The worst brings fear and doubt to mind.
The hidden best is hard to find.

MR JOHN HARRIS, of Perth, passed this heart-warming tale on to me.

Two little girls, both about five years old, live with their mother in Perth. Their father is captain of an oil tanker, which means, of course, that he is away from home for many months at a time. That, as Mr Harris says, must surely be an eternity in the life of any child—but the family have found a way of bridging the miles that separate them.

Every night just before they go to bed, the two wee girls go with their mother into the sitting-room. There hangs a big, smiling picture of their daddy —and, together, they stand before it, look up at him, and say good-night just as if he were really there.

At the same time, on the oil tanker ploughing its way through the Persian Gulf or across the Atlantic hundreds of miles away, the captain is looking at a photograph of the two little girls who are all the world to him, picturing them as they trot happily off to bed, and whispering his own good-night to them . . .

I don't think there is anything in this world more truly blessed than the family bond.

FRIDAY—JANUARY 23.

DID you hear about the man who was asked by a friend how business was going ? " Trade looking up ?" inquired the friend.

" Definitely," replied the shop-owner. " Can't help looking up—it's flat on its back now."

It may be a grim joke, but there's a hint of philosophy in it.

SATURDAY—JANUARY 24.

THERE'S a story about a poor woman who was bothered about many things, and at last ventured, timidly, to call on the minister.

She was asked in, and looked across at his elderly, pleasant face and friendly eyes. And when he asked her to tell him all about it, she lost her nervousness and told him.

And she kept on telling him, encouraged by the way he nodded with evident interest, or slowly shook his head as if deeply concerned.

And at last, suddenly conscious that she had been there a long time, she stood up and said with a new ring in her voice :

" There now, that's more than enough about me. Thank you for your help and advice. I'll be getting home now. Thank you again !"

So the minister smiled her out . . . having said nothing !

It is a very good thing to be able to talk, but often it's an even better thing to be able to listen—to listen patiently and sympathetically.

SUNDAY—JANUARY 25.

A GOOD name is rather to be chosen than great riches.

THE FRIENDSHIP BOOK

MONDAY—JANUARY 26.

I DON'T think it's too much to say that Mrs Lambert's budgie made life worthwhile for her. If she was down in the dumps, wee Jocky's cheery chirping soon made her smile again. If she was lonely, she could speak to him—and she did.

Then one day while she was cleaning the cage, the budgie flew out, landed on the edge of the water tank, overbalanced, and fell in. Poor Mrs Lambert didn't know what to do, so she rushed. across the road to the butcher's shop for help. The butcher boys came at once, but it was too late . . .

What a blow it was for the old soul. The house didn't seem to be the same without Jocky, and she could hardly even bear to look at the empty cage.

But, early that evening, there was a knock at the door. It was the two butcher boys, Murray Bain and John Hunter, with a cardboard box, from which came the sounds of chirping.

Yes, it was a new budgie! The boys were so upset by Mrs Lambert's distress that they and the manager decided to buy her another one. As it happened, when the man who breeds budgies heard why the boys wanted it, he wouldn't take a penny from them. And when they presented the budgie to Mrs Lambert, and popped it into the cage, she was quite overcome.

It's nice to hear a story with a happy ending!

TUESDAY—JANUARY 27.

THESE sermons-at-a-glance are not new; but they will always bear thinking about.

" *If you are too busy to pray—you are too busy.*"

" *Horse sense is what keeps horses from betting on men.*"

" *Never make your living at the expense of your life.*"

WEDNESDAY—JANUARY 28.

WHENEVER I feel happy,
As now and then I do,
I simply long that others
May find life pleasant, too.
And though this world is very sad
I'm glad that, now and then, I'm glad!

THURSDAY—JANUARY 29.

IF you think that stories like that of Robert Bruce and the spider don't happen nowadays, you're wrong!

When young Ian Donnan left school, his dream was to become a doctor. Alas, he didn't get a place at university and it seemed he'd have to find another job. But Ian was still set on being a doctor, so he left his home in Sunderland and went to work in a Surrey hospital as a male nurse.

It was hard and demanding, but as he worked, Ian knew he was learning much that would help him when and if he ever became a doctor. Despite his long hours and night work, he kept up his studies, passing not only his nursing exams, but also those which took him a step nearer his great wish.

He passed his nursing finals, and later he married a bonnie young nurse who worked in the same hospital. After their wedding, they went north to a Newcastle hospital, and Ian again applied for a place at university.

At long last his application was successful, and he took his place at Manchester University. There are many hurdles to cross on the way to becoming a doctor, but who can doubt that, like the story of Bruce's spider, Ian's will be a battle that must end in success?

FRIDAY—JANUARY 30.

ONE evening the American poet, Vachel Lindsay, found himself far from home, hungry, and without a dime to pay for food or shelter.

Halting at a ramshackle cottage, he was made instantly welcome by the farmworker. "You may stay, and welcome," said the labourer, "if you're willing to put up with what we've got." Man and wife gave him food and a shakedown; and he delighted the hospitable couple by reciting many of his own poems.

Next day Lindsay went on his way, but before he left he said, "You have nothing, and have given me half of it—and both of us have had an abundance."

Makes you think, doesn't it?

SATURDAY—JANUARY 31.

I EXPECT that, like myself, you know and love the song "When You Come To The End Of A Perfect Day." It was written 60 years ago by an American woman, Carrie Jacobs Bond.

Most of us know the first two verses, but few realise there is a third, unpublished verse. It seems that, soon after Carrie wrote the song, her beloved husband died, and in memory of him she wrote—

Though we part at the end of a perfect day,
And years since we met intervene,
We can cherish the joy of that perfect day
As we think of what might have been;
While God knows best why our paths must part
And one takes the lonely way,
Still we pray, hand in hand in that perfect land,
We may walk in God's perfect way.

It is a lovely farewell of thanksgiving and faith, and I am proud to pass it on to you.

FEBRUARY

THE Lord is my light and my salvation ; whom shall I fear?

IT sounded so simple when Jean said it, smiling.

A few of us were at a get-together in Jean's house; and (not really surprisingly) her mother became the topic of conversation, all of us hoping she would soon be feeling better, all of us agreeing that we couldn't help loving her.

" Well," said Jean, smiling, as I say, but with a touch of loving pride, " it's because she thinks of others that we can't help thinking of her."

It sounded so simple . . . but what a profound remark it really was.

THE Bible says—Be of good cheer.
You should love your neighbour as yourself.
Pray for them that despitefully use you.
Forgive your enemies.
Let not your heart be troubled.

I often read these words—and many others also —and when I do I recall a serious word by that humorist, Mark Twain. He said, " Most people are bothered by those passages of Scripture which they cannot understand. I always notice that the passages of Scripture which trouble me most are those I do understand."

He's right. We understand some of these Bible injunctions only too well. They are plain indeed, but acting on them is a very different thing . . .

WEDNESDAY—FEBRUARY 4.

*SO many things depress us all
     In dull or sunny weather;
But each has lots of happy things,
     When taken all together.
If you feel down, look in life's cup,
And count the things that cheer you up!*

THURSDAY—FEBRUARY 5.

HERE'S to the " Gay Queen " and her jolly skipper.

The " Gay Queen," I hasten to add, has nothing to do with Francis Gay. She's a trim little pleasure craft that sails from Rothesay three times a day, carrying holidaymakers on a cruise up the coast.

But the skipper, Herbert McIvor, does far more than simply stand at the wheel and guide the vessel. He has a fine, tenor voice—and as the " Gay Queen " cruises along, he sings appropriate songs.

Let me tell you about one trip. When they passed Dunoon, Herbert sang, " Bonnie Mary O' Argyle "; sailing up Loch Striven, he launched into " These Are My Mountains, This is My Glen "; as the passengers caught a glimpse of the towering peak of Ben Lomond, he sang " By Yon Bonnie Banks "; and there were many more. Then, as the " Gay Queen " returned to harbour, Herbert finished with " Sweet Rothesay Bay."

What the passengers didn't know was that once Herbert planned to make singing his life. For two years he studied music in Glasgow. Then came the war—and that was that. Afterwards, he went to help his father at Rothesay harbour.

But I'm sure all who sail with Herbert would agree that, even if his dream had come true, his songs couldn't bring more pleasure to more folk.

FRIDAY—FEBRUARY 6.

WHEN Mr Joseph Maxwell, of Hemel Hempstead retired, he had spent 42 years of his life as a teacher. Not only in schools of the usual kind, but in borstals and approved schools, too.

There is much I could tell you about him, and of the many ways in which he helped thousands of boys to face manhood. But I think all this is summed up in the inscription on a silver salver presented to him by his former pupils:—

> Respected as a man,
> Admired as a teacher,
> Cherished as a friend,
> And loved as a companion.

Could any man, in laying down his life's work, ask for a finer or more noble tribute ?

SATURDAY—FEBRUARY 7.

WE are living in bad times. Many of us feel that things are getting worse, and it is hardly surprising that many folk are fearful. So it is quite reassuring to find that things have been alarmingly serious before this:

In 1801, Wilberforce said: " I dare not marry, the future is so unsettled."

In 1806, William Pitt said: " There is scarcely anything around us but ruin and despair."

In 1848, Lord Shaftesbury said: " Nothing can save the British Empire from shipwreck."

In 1849, Disraeli said: " In industry, commerce and agriculture there is no hope."

In 1892, the dying Duke of Wellington said: " I thank God I shall be spared from seeing the consummation of ruin that is gathering about us."

So take courage.

THE HAPPY WORKER

Happy the man whose work is set
Where tree and hill and cloud are met;
In toil who pleasure can discern
And each day something new can learn.

DAVID HOPE

WINTER EVENING

There's a glory in the winter,
When the ice is carved like stone,
And the parting rays of sunshine
Gleam like radiance from His throne;
Now, the wind has shrunk to silence,
And the frost begins to bite,
And soon from ridge and corrie,
Will roll down the shades of night.

DAVID HOPE

SUNDAY—FEBRUARY 8.

THE Kingdom of God is within you.

MONDAY—FEBRUARY 9.

THE lady felt for some time that her house-keeper had been reading some of her private correspondence; something no one ought to do. But she did not want to lose the housekeeper, who had many excellent qualities, and so the lady decided to take advantage of the situation. So she wrote to a friend, " My housekeeper is quite wonderful, but there are certain things I wish she would do." And, believe it or not, there was immediately a vast change for the better !

They say that eavesdroppers never hear any good of themselves, but good came of it in this case. And it was a most tactful way of bringing about an improvement. I'm not so sure that our most " frank " friends, who blurt out the truth to our faces, always get the best results.

TUESDAY—FEBRUARY 10.

I EXPECT you heard long ago about the minister and his farmer friend George ? They say George was normally a very cheerful member of the kirk; but one afternoon he looked more serious than the minister had ever seen him before. A little anxious, therefore, the minister remarked—" You look uncommonly sad, George ?. Is anything wrong ?"

" Got a new hat," was the reply.

" A new hat ? Why, if anything, I should think that a cause for rejoicing."

" Aye, maybe so, minister," said George, his face as dismal as ever. " Trouble is, sir, every time I laugh, it falls off."

WEDNESDAY—FEBRUARY 11.

IT'S never easy climbing hills,
And if the road is steep,
Some folk soon weary, or turn back,
Or simply go to sleep!
It's only those, the gallant few.
Who gaze upon the splendid view!

THURSDAY—FEBRUARY 12.

IN the town of Windsor, Ontario, on the other side of the Atlantic, lives a friendly Salvationist called Mary Atherton.

Mary is getting on in years, and, though she makes light of her troubles, I know her health is anything but good. Yet all who know her will tell you she is one of God's angels, always looking for little ways of helping folk.

It was Mary who sent me the following lines, and although she didn't say so, somehow I have the feeling they are an echo of her own way of life:—

Is anybody happier because you passed his way? Does anyone remember that you spoke to him today? The day is almost over, and its toiling time is through, is there anyone who's thinking warm and friendly thoughts of you?

Can you say tonight, in parting with the day that's slipping fast, that you helped a single brother of the many that you passed? Is a single heart rejoicing over what you did or said; does the man whose hopes were fading, now with courage look ahead?

Did you waste the day, or lose it? Was it well or badly spent? Did you leave a glow of kindness, or a scar of discontent? As you close your eyes in slumber, do you think that God will say, " You have earned another blessing by the work you did today "?

MR MOWATT, the antique dealer, looked longingly at a single pistol displayed by a trade friend in his West Highland shop. " If only it were a pair," exclaimed Mr Mowatt, " then they really would be worth something !"

" I know that," answered his friend. " You could have had this one for a tenner. That's all it's worth by itself."

Judge Mr Mowatt's delight then, a few days later, when he saw an exact replica of the pistol displayed by a Glasgow dealer. This time they wanted £20, and although it was on the dear side, Mr Mowatt paid up without a murmur. Would not the value of the complete pair of pistols go well into three figures ? At the first opportunity he went back to see about the first pistol.

" I'm sorry," said his friend; " I thought you didn't want it, so I sold it to a dealer from Glasgow !"

SATURDAY—FEBRUARY 14.

MANY of us have sung the hymn, " Break, Thou, the bread of life," and some of us know it was written by the American poet Mary Artemisia Lathbury. Few of us, however, know that Miss Lathbury—who died in 1913—founded the " Look-up Legion " based on the four rules—

Look up and not down;
Look forward, and not back;
Look out, and not in . . .
And lend a hand.

The idea of the Legion was that if more and more folk persuaded more and more folk to live in this way, the world would be a better place. She dreamed her dream a long time ago, but we could do with such dreams today.

SUNDAY—FEBRUARY 15.

SEARCH the Scriptures.

MONDAY—FEBRUARY 16.

JOHN WILLIAMSON has now retired as Chief Constable of Northampton, but he still remembers a visit he paid to a prison cell, where a man of 75 was serving a sentence. Kindly, Mr Williamson tried to reason with him about the life he had been leading. "Really, Dad," he said, "you ought to know better."

The old man looked up at him. "Son," he replied, "I know better, all right—the trouble is I can't do better."

Though the difference between knowing better and doing better may never land us in a prison cell, our lives, if we fail to recognise it, cannot but be less fine and less worthy.

TUESDAY—FEBRUARY 17.

THEY say that "fools rush in where angels fear to tread." The example I have in mind took place when someone collapsed at the kerbside.

Sir James, whose name is a household word in surgery, was passing and he asked his chauffeur to stop. Already a Boy Scout was kneeling over the unconscious figure. He felt, rather than saw, the great man approach through the crowd, and he was probably too engrossed to see the black leather case which showed his profession. Without looking up he demanded—"Have you passed an exam in First Aid?"

"I don't think I have," answered Sir James. "In that case," said the Scout, raising his hand like a traffic policeman, "stand aside!"

WEDNESDAY—FEBRUARY 18.

A SUNDOWN splendid and serene,
A child's kiss on your cheek,
A timeless moment when you're thanked—
You smile but cannot speak.
Such things are wealth beyond compare—
And compensate for grief and care.

THURSDAY—FEBRUARY 19.

ONE of the most heart-breaking tasks, I think, which most of us have to face at some time, is going through the belongings of a loved one who has gone, each one with its own precious memory.

Miss M. Gordon, of St Andrews, was faced with this task, after her mother had died. But amongst her mother's belongings Miss Gordon came across these lines, written in her mother's own hand, which did a great deal to calm and strengthen her—

If we could see beyond our present sorrow, beyond our present grief as God can see, we would be braver, knowing some tomorrow will still hold happiness for you and me.

If our blurred eyes could see beyond their weeping, the sunlit hills that some day we shall climb, we would be stronger and we would be keeping a tryst with hope through every darkened time.

If we could see beyond some fresh disaster the road smoothed out again before our eyes, we would be calmer and we would learn faster the lessons life unfolds to make us wise.

We are so blinded by a moment's sorrow, so hurt by any trouble, any pain, that we forget the joys beyond believing, the peace that will be ours some day again.

FRIDAY—FEBRUARY 20.

EXCITING, sometimes, to have a glimpse, however brief, into a child's world.

I have just heard of a little girl who told her equally little friend next door—" It's Mum's birthday. She's twenty-six."

" Gosh," exclaimed the little friend. " She's getting old !"

" She sure is," agreed the girl. " And do you know, she can still ride a bicycle !"

SATURDAY—FEBRUARY 21.

I WONDER if you have had an experience like this.

It happened to Mrs Grace Andrew, of Vancouver. Among her friends were a mother and daughter whom she was always glad to meet when out shopping. The elderly woman and her devoted daughter were always friendly, nice to talk to and pleasant to think about afterwards.

One day Mrs Andrew heard that the old lady had died. She was very sorry, and wrote to the daughter to express her sympathy. And that was that.

Some weeks later, walking in Vancouver, she turned a corner, and there, on the pavement, was the old lady's daughter, alone. Mrs Andrew had never seen the two apart; and (as she confessed) it was only in that moment that she fully realised what had happened—that death had separated two loving folk. And although she had been sorry, it was not till she saw the daughter without her mother that she was able to understand what loneliness the mother's passing had meant.

Is it not true that sometimes we don't understand what we ourselves have never experienced?

SUNDAY—FEBRUARY 22.

THE truth shall make you free.

MONDAY—FEBRUARY 23.

I SOMETIMES wish that in the English language we had some other word when we part from our friends than the somewhat formal " Good-bye." Some other languages have several words, saying this very thing, but in different ways. But in English you can hardly say " Cheerio ! Keep your chin up," when you are speaking to a bishop. There really is not much alternative to " Good-bye."

But if we think about it a little more carefully, we will remember that it is only an abbreviation of the saying, "God be with you." And what finer wish could there be as we shake hands ?"

TUESDAY—FEBRUARY 24.

IT was all of thirty years since I had stepped inside the little hotel overlooking the bay; but nothing was much changed. Looking at the familiar surroundings old memories came flooding back. How comfortable it was and how kind everyone had been ! In particular I recalled one waitress who, no matter how early my departure, roused me from sleep and sent me on my way with a splendid breakfast before anyone else was stirring.

Meantime the ownership and staff of the hotel had changed completely. No one could remember me. But I told them about my recollections of the place and at once they said, " That was Jane ! She died some years ago, but everyone still speaks about her as you do. She was a wonderful person."

Hers was a humble job, no doubt, but what better memorial could anyone wish to leave upon this earth?

WEDNESDAY—FEBRUARY 25.

A SUNNY day—you walk alone,
No more your loved one here;
How harsh the light and all things bright,
Hot tears of grief how near.
Though sad your heart, can you not smile
Because you two once walked a mile?

THURSDAY—FEBRUARY 26.

THERE is a story of an American millionaire who lost every dollar he had in the Wall Street crash, some 40 years ago.

The shock was too much for him, so he decided to make an end of things.

He went to the beach to drown himself in the sea, but as he reached the water's edge he paused. He picked up a tiny, beautiful shell—so fragile that the least pressure of his finger and thumb would have shattered it.

How, he asked himself, has this delicate wonder survived rough seas and high waves? The sea can wreck a big ship—yet a shell, light as a petal, remains unharmed. How?

Then light dawned on his agonised mind. Why, of course, the ships fight against the storm, but the shell rocks with the moving billows, offering no resistance.

With this thought in mind, the ruined millionaire turned his back on the waves, to begin a new life. Not a dramatic, strong fight against heavy odds, but co-operation with life; not a selfish way of living, but a way of thinking about others. Today the failure has won his way back to a happiness he never knew before.

P.S.—The shell at the water's edge is known as an angel's wing.

STORIES OF THE NIGHT

Who passed this way an hour ago,
Writing stories in the snow?
The skilful eye the tale may read
Of fear that lent new wings to speed
And terror striking in the night.
Now all is peace at morning light,
And glittering patterns by the stream
Show a nightmare turned to dream.

DAVID HOPE

A HOUSE BY THE SEA

There's a spot that I remember
I passed it one fine day,
So quickly, for, as travellers do
I hurried on my way.

A house, a field, a glimpse of sea,
I think I see them still,
And feel the wind that stirs at dawn
The heather on the hill.

DAVID HOPE

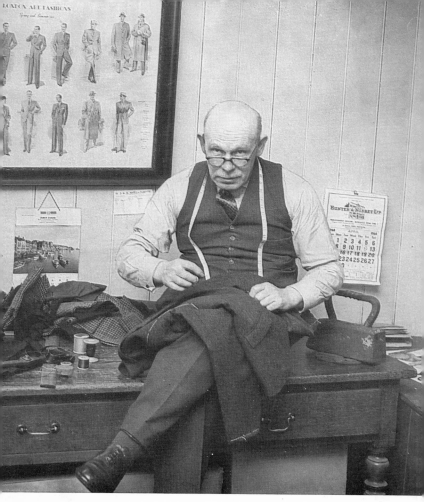

THE TAILOR

He's seen the lot — from "Oxford bags"
To legs of drainpipe measure ;
Plus-eights and half-forgotten fads
In which men once took pleasure.

Though vogues and fashions come and go
This man we'll always need,
With skilful hands to cut the cloth
And test a piece of tweed.

DAVID HOPE

FRIDAY—FEBRUARY 27.

FOR a long time Minnie Hall, a patient in a hospital at Perth, had one great desire.

I doubt if you could guess what it was. Not a day by the sea or a car trip to the hills; not to go shopping; not to escape from hospital.

Bless her, Minnie wanted to feel the rain on her face. You see, she was not allowed out when there was a chance of rain. If she were in her wheelchair in the grounds and a cloud came over the blue sky, she was hurriedly wheeled in.

But then at last, one day when Minnie was out, a shower came on suddenly, and she lifted her face and felt its cold, thrilling touch and it was heaven to Minnie.

Think of her next time you grumble about a heavy shower.

SATURDAY—FEBRUARY 28.

DURING the war, Albert Norman, a London jeweller who spent all his spare time among his roses, was seeking the perfect red rose. He tried again and again until, at long last, his patience was rewarded.

Proudly he took a seedling rose bearing a red bloom to his friend, William Harkness, a great judge of roses and a genius at growing them. Albert had named it after William. But as William looked at its beauty he knew there was only one name for it—not his own, but that of his beloved wife, Ena.

From that one plant have come all the millions of Ena Harkness roses that are grown today all over the world—and in countless gardens that rose still speaks of William's love for Ena—a perfect tribute from a husband to a wife.

MARCH

FREELY ye have received, freely give.

Monday—March 2.

THERE'S a story that once Satan announced he was retiring from business, and that all the tools of his trade were up for sale.

On the day of the sale, a long line of jars stood on a table, each labelled and priced. In one jar was jealousy. In another was hate. In a third was pride. In the others were deceit, malice, greed, selfishness, and all the ruses and wiles of Satan.

But, a little apart from the rest, was another jar, smaller than the others and almost empty. Yet, it was priced higher than all the others put together.

" Why ?" someone asked.

" Because," said Satan, " one pinch of that inside a man and he is mine. I can use him in any way that suits my purpose. It is almost finished, because I have used it on nearly everyone—but few know that it belongs to me."

The jar was labelled " *Discouragement.*"

Tuesday—March 3.

IT was the end of the amateur drama festival, and the adjudicator was trying to hint to a local group that in attempting Shakespeare's *Macbeth* they had perhaps bitten off more than they could chew.

" You know," he said, " many of the world's leading actresses have found it very difficult to play the part of Lady Macbeth."

" Is that so ?" inquired the young lady who had just completed the part. " Well, I found it no bother at all."

WEDNESDAY—MARCH 4.

IF in the street you chance to meet
Someone you know, just smile.
Then ask her how she is, and wait—
No doubt, she'll talk awhile.
This simple trick will, ere you part,
Keep friendship rich and warm your heart.

THURSDAY—MARCH 5.

I WOULD like to tell you about one of the most beautiful weddings I have ever attended. The church was decorated with roses and chrysanthemums of every shade. The bride was radiant, and her wedding dress, declared the Lady of the House, was a dream. Indeed, as the bride and 'groom stepped down the aisle, we felt that we had never seen such a fine-looking couple.

Yet, amid all this joy, there was more than a hint of sadness. For the bride's mother, the one to whom (apart from the couple themselves) all this meant most of all, saw nothing of it. Eight or nine years before, while her daughter was still at school, she began to lose her sight, and before long she was completely blind.

So, on her only child's wedding day, she could only imagine what the rest of us were seeing . . . the loveliness of the bride; the pride on her husband's face as he led their daughter to the altar; and the couple's joy as the wedding march pealed forth at the end of the service.

It is, perhaps, the most precious dream of any mother—that one day she will stand in church and see her daughter married. It is a dream that, for this mother, was never to come true, and I only pray that, in some secret way, it was given to her to share in the joy that was so rightfully hers.

FRIDAY—MARCH 6.

YOU have no doubt seen many a blue-and-white willow pattern plate, but do you know the story of the design?

It shows a garden and a river spanned by a quaint bridge. There are three (sometimes four) figures on the bridge. There is a tiny ship, and two doves.

The story is that Koong-Shee, a lovely Chinese girl, was in love with Chang, one of her rich father's servants. When ordered to marry a wealthy suitor, Koong-Shee refused, so her father locked her in a shed. Somehow she got a message to Chang—"Gather your blossom before it is stolen," and he carried her off. We see the lovers crossing the bridge, the irate father following with a whip.

The lovers sailed off in a ship, spending a night in a hut on an island, but they were surprised by the father, who set the hut on fire. Koong-Shee and Chang perished in the flames, but at dawn their spirits rose in the form of doves, and they winged their way to the islands of the blessed.

It seems to me that every willow pattern plate preaches a sermon: Evil may conquer in a material sense, but always love itself is victorious.

SATURDAY—MARCH 7.

I LIKE this little story of Mischa Elman, the famous Russian violinist.

When he was 70, and about to begin a European concert tour, he remarked to a friend—"When I first played in public at the age of twelve, people used to say, '*Isn't he wonderful for his age*?'" Then, with a rare twinkle, he added, "Trouble is they are beginning to say it again."

What if you are growing old? Life can still be fun!

SUNDAY—MARCH 8.

IN all labour there is profit.

MONDAY—MARCH 9.

I CAME on a snail today. He was looking most handsome, with his golden-brown shell gleaming in the sunlight. But this elegant fellow was lost. He had crossed a concrete pavement and was now heading for an area made entirely of asphalt. So I put him back in bit of rough grass where he would surely be safer and happier.

If a gardener had seen me, he might not have been too pleased, but it wasn't near to anyone's garden. I was thinking in any case about all the asphalt jungles which man creates, making life so much harder for all his humble neighbours on this planet. The least we can do is to give them a helping hand whenever we have the chance.

TUESDAY—MARCH 10.

ONE day Mr Sam Baird was driving into town. The rain was pelting down. Suddenly, at a bus stop, he saw a boy of about twelve in a school blazer, with no coat, getting well and truly soaked. Mr Baird pulled up and wound down his window. "Can I give you a lift into town?" he asked.

"Thank you, sir," replied the boy politely, "but I'm sorry I don't know you well enough."

It was, perhaps, an unexpected answer. But as Mr Baird drove off with a wave, far from feeling slighted, he was full of admiration for the laddie's courtesy and firmness—and for the wisdom of the parents who had shown their boy how to cope with what has become, unhappily, a difficult problem for youngsters today.

WEDNESDAY—MARCH 11.

I OFTEN feel depressed because
There's much to harass one.
Some days the bairns just get me down—
I feel I can't keep on.
But when I've had a little sit,
I do the chores, and sing a bit!

THURSDAY—MARCH 12.

THIS story began 50 years ago when a Glasgow mother died, leaving her husband with a family of six to bring up.

Her name was Mrs Dale, and her youngest child, Jimmy, was only two. Being the youngest, Jimmy missed his mother most, and his dad did all he could to make up for it.

As the years passed and Jimmy grew to manhood, he vowed he'd make up for all his dad had done for him, and he was better than his word.

Even when Jimmy married, he still remembered his promise. Every night when he finished work, instead of going straight home he went round to see his dad, now living alone. He took him the evening paper and made sure the fire was built up for the night. Then he set off to his own house.

Oh, nothing would have made him happier than to give his dad a home. But old Mr Dale was sturdily independent. He liked his own little house. So Jim, bless him, did the next best thing—and for 17 years, apart from his annual holiday, he never once missed seeing his dad every night.

His long mission is over now. Mr Dale passed away at the age of 82. I know Jim would say his greatest blessing was to have a good father—and it was a blessing for which he gave thanks in the finest way of all.

FRIDAY—MARCH 13.

I CAME home early the other evening and surprised my wife, who was writing a letter.

I just couldn't help catching sight of the first two or three lines—"Dear Jim, I've heard such wonderful things about you   "

So I asked the Lady of the House what she was up to, and she explained she had been visiting one of her old dears in an eventide home.

" She is very sweet and content," she told me. " Not too well these days, though. Still, every week since her son and his wife went to Canada, she has written to them—never failed, even when it cost a bit of effort. But she had a fall last week and sprained her wrist, so she asked me to write the news to her son. I'm doing that now. Tomorrow I'll show her the letter, and she can tell me if it's suitable. The great thing is not to worry her son —so I'm going to make light of the fall and be sure to say she'll be writing as usual next week !"

It all sounds trivial—but what a big thing to that gallant granny !

SATURDAY—MARCH 14.

LESSONS were not going well. The young lady teacher was almost in despair with a somewhat slow class. Was not H.M. Inspector of Schools due the very next day ? Finally she exclaimed— " Well, I've done all I can with you and I cannot do any more. When the inspector comes tomorrow, you can at least all try to look intelligent. Sit up, try to look interested, put up your hand if you think he's not going to point the question at you even if you don't know the answers you can help me by trying to look as if you did !"

SUNDAY—MARCH 15.

YE shall be as gods, knowing good and evil.

MONDAY—MARCH 16.

A FRIEND stopped me in the street a day or two ago. He's turned eighty, but he's still lively. With a rare twinkle in his eyes he asked me a question—" Say," he said, " what's easier than falling out of bed?"

I thought there was a catch somewhere. " Tell me," I asked.

" Being sorry for yourself when you do." Then away he strode, leaving me thinking.

I am not going to say the man I met is right all along the line, but he did remind me that it is indeed very easy to feel sorry for yourself. The least thing wrong can set you going downhill.

You become convinced that you're unfortunate, and you feel tragically unhappy. It's so easy to get into this mood. Easier than falling out of bed.

TUESDAY—MARCH 17.

I HEAR that two men walked along a street in a Staffordshire town one morning, talking as they walked, oblivious to the crowds. Both were good-looking, both neatly dressed. One was a miner, the other a lord. They called each other by their christian names.

The odd thing was that most of the people in the street recognised the two men, although the lord didn't think of his pal as a miner, and the miner never addressed his friend as " your lordship."

They had been lads at school together—and they were equals because friends.

BUILDING THE LINER

Add this man's skill to that man's strength
Till the liner's built at length.
So runs through life this ancient tale —
"We" succeed where "I" must fail.

C

DAVID HOPE

SPRING BLOSSOMS

*You can smell a Channel garden
In a bunch for half-a-crown,
And instead of city buses,
See the little bays run down
To coves where waves come lapping,
On a breezy April day —
Oh the tulips and the lilies,
How they steal my heart away !*

DAVID HOPE

WEDNESDAY—MARCH 18.

WHEN sad of heart and burdened with
A grief you can't forget,
How can you, in your anguish, cease
In bitterness to fret?
But if you find some tasks to do,
What comfort they may bring to you.

THURSDAY—MARCH 19.

IN Janefield Cemetery, Glasgow, there is a gravestone with three names on it.

One is of a soldier called Robert Rankin. The second is of his brother Archie. Beneath them appears the name " Yapp Singh."

How it came to be there is a strange and moving tale. Yapp Singh was a Chinese waif who was given a home by a Scots couple in Hong Kong. When they came back to Scotland over 30 years ago, Yapp Singh, now a young man, came too.

As the years passed, the kindly Scots couple who had looked after him for so long grew old and ill. They knew Yapp Singh had no one of his own to remember him, so they asked their minister, Rev. Andrew Rankin, if he would look after him when they had gone. Mr Rankin gave them his word, and when they died he wrote regularly to Yapp Singh, almost as if he were one of his own family.

Then Yapp Singh himself died. Since he was alone in the world, he was going to be laid in an unmarked grave. But Mr Rankin heard about it, and, remembering his promise made so long ago, he decided that Yapp Singh, once a Chinese orphan, should lie in his own family grave, where he himself will one day be laid. That is why today the name of Yapp Singh stands on that memorial as the proof of a promise that was honoured to the end.

FRIDAY—MARCH 20.

I CAN'T tell you why he was in prison, and it wouldn't be fair to give his name.

Let me say simply that he is an Ayrshire man whose wrong-doing earned him a long term of imprisonment. While he was there he read of the faithfulness of an R.A.F. officer's dog, which remembered him after an absence of four years.

The prisoner couldn't help wondering if his Labrador dog would remember him after such a long time. After all, he thought, his former friends didn't want to know him. Why should a dog?

At last the day arrived when he stepped outside the prison gates. Alone, he made his way home and opened the door of his house. With a bark of excitement his dog threw itself at him, licking his hands and face and jumping with joy.

Then the dog turned and trotted off—only to come back, proudly bearing his slippers, almost as if to say, " Welcome home—and please don't go away again !"

Does a dog see the real you? Some folk believe so. But whatever the answer, surely the devotion and trust in the eyes of that dog would make his master want to be a better man.

SATURDAY—MARCH 21.

THERE are some folk, aren't there, who seem to delight in picking faults in others? One such lady is said to have greeted Dr Samuel Johnson after he had carried through the tremendous task of preparing the first English Dictionary—" I see, Dr Johnson," she complained, " that you have included many naughty words in your Dictionary."

" That's perfectly true, madam," he answered, " and I see that you have been looking for them !"

SUNDAY—MARCH 22.

SEE that ye fall not out by the way.

MONDAY—MARCH 23.

I LIKE this story told about the Duke of Edinburgh.

A few years ago when the Queen and her husband were in the U.S.A., the two of them visited a supermarket. As they walked down one of the aisles a fussy woman said to the Duke—"Don't you know you should walk two steps behind the Queen?"

With his whimsical smile the Duke replied, "You are right, madam. But I think it's all right this time. You see, yesterday the Queen and I sat side by side watching a football match . . . and we became quite chummy!"

TUESDAY—MARCH 24.

ONE of the old ladies of whom for years my wife has thought much, and has always enjoyed visiting, has passed on recently, and my wife has been looking through the autograph album the old lady delighted to show her visitors.

Two pages of that old book seem to have got stuck together. Carefully the Lady of the House separated the pages. One was blank. On the other was a single sentence written over sixty years ago. Now, looking back, my wife feels that the challenge of this short sentence must have remained with " her " old lady all through life, for she was intensely happy in spite of poverty, always remarkably content, always easily pleased. Both of us think the old dear must have put this one sentence into practice every day she lived:—*Wise folk care nothing for what they cannot have.*

THE FRIENDSHIP BOOK

IN spite of some annoyance,
Of having much to do,
Of little disappointments
And just a sigh or two,
How good if you at eve can say—
" It's been a very happy day !"

THURSDAY—MARCH 26.

THE Lady of the House doesn't agree with me, but I can't think of any woman who can resist a bargain. And here's a story to prove it.

One Sunday, when the crab boats landed their catch at a fishing village, they were besieged by buyers.

One woman on her way to church didn't want to miss a bargain, but she didn't want to miss church, either. How could she do both ? Well, trust a woman. She bought a lovely big crab and tied it in a headsquare. At the church she discreetly placed the bundle under her pew until she could take it home after the service.

It's what anybody might do without dreaming what would happen next . . .

During a hymn she became aware of a slight commotion in the pews. She looked round—and, my goodness, there was her gay headsquare, with a big knot on top, ambling slowly down the aisle ! When she'd tucked her purchase under the pew she'd forgotten that the crab was still very much alive.

A dilemma indeed, but it was met with perfect feminine composure. For the woman just went on singing without batting an eye and pretended the mysterious, crawling headsquare had nothing to do with her !

FRIDAY—MARCH 27.

IT did taste good.

It reminded me of my boyhood days—coming home from school and sniffing (even as I opened the door) the warm smell of new-baked bread, and seeing the loaves, crisp and appetising, on the table.

I remembered my mother saying there was potted meat or jam to spread on the bread at tea, and how I tucked into the slices, light and soft but with crispy, flaky edges, and how I begged for the crust, and spread butter over and ate it without anything else because it was delicious that way.

But why such memories in days when you buy a sliced loaf neatly wrapped from the shop?

Simply because the other day a schoolboy knocked at our door, saying, " Mrs McArthur asked me to bring you this, and she says she hopes you enjoy it."

It was a warm, nut-brown loaf, and the Lady of the House and I enjoyed it at tea-time. All the more so because it was baked by a neighbour who will be 86 next birthday!

Yes, it *did* taste good!

SATURDAY—MARCH 28.

AN American friend in a letter tells the story of an explanation given by one very small pupil to another.

A teacher of children aged six had given out sheets of coloured paper. Then she told her class to cut out shapes, adding—" And you must share the scissors as we have only one pair for each desk."

" What does share mean?" one pupil asked the boy next to him.

In a whisper came the reply—" Share is what you do with the scissors when teacher's looking."

SUNDAY—MARCH 29.

AND Jesus said unto him, "Verily I say unto thee, today shalt thou be with me in paradise."

MONDAY—MARCH 30.

HERE'S an Easter story I may have told you before, but one which I think well worth repeating. It takes place somewhere in England.

The church was filled to capacity on Easter Sunday morning; and after the sermon the minister added a few kindly and impromptu remarks.

"My friends," he began, "it is a delight to see so many strange faces in the congregation this morning. I welcome you one and all; and if it should happen that I do not see some of you again until next Easter, I take this opportunity of wishing you a very Merry Christmas and a happy New Year!"

I wouldn't like to swear this is a true story. But it is certainly a valid comment on the fact that more and more people, especially young ones, are losing the habit of regular church attendance.

We must find out why — and do our best to put the matter right.

TUESDAY—MARCH 31.

FOR those executives who are growing sleek and are rather full of their own importance, I recommend a story of Henry Ford. Whenever there was a problem to iron out, he did not send for accountants or foremen or mechanics or sales managers. *He went to see them.*

When asked why he did it that way round, he explained, "It saves time. I can get away from the other feller a lot faster than he can leave me."

APRIL

IT'S little things that get you down—
Life's pinpricks and vexations,
Its daily, petty ills and cares,
Its nagging, stark frustrations.
Yet happy, precious little things
Give tired spirits golden wings!

A YOUNG man left Glasgow to find his fortune in Canada. He was an only son, and before he went he promised faithfully to write to his mother. Alas, the letters grew fewer as time passed, and at length they stopped altogether. His mother hid her worry and sadness behind a smile, and if folk asked about him, there was never a hint of bitterness in her reply.

Then, many years later, a letter arrived at last. Yes, it was from her son, and he was staying somewhere in his old home town. He told her he was deeply ashamed of himself—so much so, that he'd quite understand if she never wanted to see him again. If that was how she felt, he would not come home. But if she would forgive him, he asked her to hang a sheet on the back-green line, as a sign.

Next morning he set out for his mother's house, wondering what he would find. As he rounded the last corner, his eyes filled with tears—for every sheet in the house was hanging out on the line!

It was his mother's way of telling him he was not only forgiven, but that a thousand welcomes awaited him.

It is, I think, one of the loveliest parables of mother love I have ever come across.

FRIDAY—APRIL 3.

MRS MONAGHAN, of Jarrow, is in her thirties, a cheerful housewife who's always thinking of others. Every day she spends longer on her knees than most women for, because of an illness, she cannot walk and it is the only way she can get around the house.

Fortunately she has that rare kind of courage that always makes the best of things. And there's so much she can do in all the humble chores that help to create a happy home.

For a woman kneels to scrub the doorstep, so it may welcome all who call; to kindle the fire that cheers the family on a cold winter night; to bath the baby, to tie a boy's shoelace before he sets off for school, even to plant seeds in the garden. And, at the end of the day, she kneels to give thanks for the home which is the centre of her world.

Fanciful? Perhaps. But, on their knees, the women of this world do blessed work, and I'm sure Mrs Monaghan is no exception.

SATURDAY—APRIL 4.

SOME time ago I received a postcard. On it was a poem written by Mrs Elizabeth Gozney, of Berkhamsted—and I found it so appealing that I promised myself I would pass it on. I think you, too, will find that it will charm you back to childhood for a moment :—

Look through the eyes of a child and you'll see
The rainbow in bubbles, a bird flying free;
To chase butterflies in the dew on bare feet,
Find a new friend in each kitten you meet;
To ponder the magical shape of a rose,
Watch a kite in the breeze as it blows;
To share in the world of a child's little day
Is to find happiness that endures through life's way.

THE FRIENDSHIP BOOK

SUNDAY—APRIL 5.

ON the day of prosperity be joyful, but in the day of adversity consider.

MONDAY—APRIL 6.

A LETTER from Mrs Calder, of Perth, reminded me of these lines which I came across many years ago—

Courtesy is the eye which overlooks your friend's broken gate. Neighbourliness is the hand which helps him to mend it.

It prompts me to ask which you think is the more blessed—to pretend politely that something doesn't exist or, in the friendliest possible way, to set about putting it right?

TUESDAY—APRIL 7.

I WOULD like to pass on a story so old that perhaps you have forgotten it. It is a story told by a Border doctor, and it reminds us of the canny ways of sheep dogs, especially those trained by Scottish shepherds, and treated by them as if they were human beings.

While visiting a shepherd's home one day, the doctor talked with the elderly man whose three sheep dogs lay stretched before the kitchen fire, all sound asleep. When the shepherd offered to accompany the doctor a short distance, he gave a whistle. Instantly two of the dogs were on their feet. But the third did not stir. " Strange," remarked the doctor as men and dogs left the house, " that the other dog doesn't come with us."

" No, no, it's not strange at all," replied the shepherd. " He knows it's not his turn—he was out on the hills all morning."

WEDNESDAY—APRIL 8.

OF course you have a good excuse
For grumbling night and day.
This old world is a sorry place—
You tread a lonely way.
But moans don't make life's fog less thick;
It's sunny smiles that do the trick!

THURSDAY—APRIL 9.

ON holiday at Hartlepool, Mr and Mrs Davison, of Dumbarton, set out for a walk along the promenade, while the waves broke in clouds of spray against the 50-foot high sea wall.

On the wall, looking down into the grey depths, stood a woman in her fifties. As they passed, Mr Davison called out a greeting. The woman turned in surprise, for she thought she was alone—and a moment later she burst into tears.

She told Mr and Mrs Davison that her only son had been killed when his plane crashed. Then, two years ago, her husband died. Life alone had become too much for her. When Mr Davison spoke to her she had been on the point of ending it all . . .

Mr and Mrs Davison comforted her and took her back to their hotel for tea. Quietly they assured her that others needed her, even though her own family had gone. That night she left for home, full of gratitude and ready for a fresh start.

In the weeks that followed, the Davisons often thought of her—then, a few months later, a card arrived in the post bearing a picture of two hands clasped in prayer. They knew it was a message from the woman to say all was still well.

I wonder when you last spoke a friendly word to a stranger? It may not save a life—but who knows what else it could mean?

FRIDAY—APRIL 10.

APPARENTLY a very cranky and short-tempered man bought one of those hearing-aids which are virtually invisible.

A few days after having the aid fitted and adjusted, the crotchety old fellow called to thank the specialist who had supplied the gadget. " I like it," declared the utterly satisfied customer.

" And I'll bet your family likes it, too," said the specialist.

" Oh," chuckled the deaf man, " they still don't know I've got it, and I'm having a whale of a time! Already I've changed my will three times."

SATURDAY—APRIL 11.

THE little white dog was injured in a road accident and brought to the vet's surgery, without a collar, certainly without a pedigree, and now, apparently, without a home. Day after day the vet worked to bring him back to life and health. But the little dog was disinterested in life, turning away his head when offered food; listening to every footfall that came into the outer office.

Meantime the police were searching for the owner, and so one day there came a familiar step and the sound of children's voices outside. At last the little white dog rose to his feet, his head cocked on one side, listening eagerly, his tail wagging furiously. In a moment he was reunited with those he loved, setting all the human beings round about an example in loyalty and affection.

SUNDAY—APRIL 12.

FROM the rising of the sun unto the going down of the same the Lord's name is to be praised.

THE FRIENDSHIP BOOK

MONDAY—APRIL 13.

IT would be eight o'clock when the Lady of the House joined me in the living-room.

"Sorry," she sighed as she sat in her chair. "I seem to have had no end of things to do. I felt I must tidy up and do some vacuuming, especially as there'll be no chance tomorrow. I've earned a rest!"

She was tired—and no wonder. She had been on the go all day, and here it was after eight at night.

Then she said, unexpectedly, "Oh, well, I'm glad I don't live in Buckingham Palace. It has three miles of corridors carpeted in crimson! Francis, it makes me tired to think of it—fancy beginning to vacuum that vast area, not to mention dusting and vacuuming six hundred rooms! Goodness!"

After that I think the Lady of the House felt better. There's something to be said for a house without three miles of carpet!

TUESDAY—APRIL 14.

GORDON SLATER (not his real name) was once a company director; but alas! He lost his job after his company was "taken over."

"At least," I said to him one day, "it would mean a golden handshake for you."

He answered, "More like a copper handshake!"

He runs a small driving school nowadays, which could be rather tame after the big decisions he once made and his journeys all over the world. But this is not how Gordon Slater sees it. "I've just pushed Mrs Anderson through her driving test," he told me in an excited voice. "Her husband has a thrombosis. She is 69 and she has never driven. I must admit it took about 69 lessons!"

It's an example for us all—whatever you are doing, do it well!

WEDNESDAY—APRIL 15.

I COULD, if I cared, count the folk
Who've failed me or taken me in,
Bad neighbours, false friends, and the like—
Much wiser, however, to grin.
Such knaves simply make me see red.
I'll count up my angels instead!

THURSDAY—APRIL 16.

I'M afraid I spilled the salt at dinner the other day.

The Lady of the House (who pretends to be superstitious, but isn't really) stood over me while, dutifully, I picked some up and threw it over my left shoulder. Then, with honour and the gods satisfied, we carried on with our meal.

But I was glad, in a way, that I spilled the salt—and that my wife, like most women, enjoys these wee superstitions. For it made me ask why spilling salt should be bad luck—and in my efforts to find the answer, I stumbled across something rather interesting.

It concerns Leonardo da Vinci's famous painting of the Last Supper. You are sure to have heard of the masterpiece, depicting Jesus sitting in the centre at a long table, his disciples on either side of Him. He has just told them that one of them will betray Him, and, horrified, they are asking Him and each other who the traitor will be.

At first it seems there is nothing in the picture to give the answer. But if you look closely at it, you will see the figure of Judas accidentally knocking over the salt cellar with his elbow.

Was that the start of the superstition? I cannot say. But I'll remember that picture of Judas and I know you will, too.

FRIDAY—APRIL 17.

ONE of Scotland's deepest and most provocative thinkers was Thomas Carlyle. He was also a great and delightful letter-writer.

As countless folk know, the house in which he was born still stands in Ecclefechan. There, if we will, we can see intimate items which once belonged to this famous writer and philosopher, including some of his letters.

It is long since a friend of mine visited the Carlyle Museum, and I dare say the little friendly caretaker of those days has passed on. It was she who paid one of the loveliest of all tributes to Thomas Carlyle. She remarked to my old friend, " Och, my sight is not so good now, but I always dust the show-cases with ma specs off—I'd no' get through my day's work if I was to begin reading them."

SATURDAY—APRIL 18.

THIS is no more than a passing thought found in a delightful scrap-book full of such thoughts, and sent to me by Joan Reed, of Bath.

But I found this one challenging, offering a new slant on, of all things, revenge ! Here it is :—

Why, when we hear so often of people trying to get even with those who've done them wrong or hurt, do we never hear (or speak) of trying to get even with others who have helped us or done us a kindness ?

Now that kind of revenge really can be sweet !

SUNDAY—APRIL 19.

COME, let us sing unto the Lord : let us make a joyful noise to the rock of our salvation.

MONDAY—APRIL 20.

ONE summer day, Mr Arnold Lewis, of Burnside, Kendal, went for a car run with his son to the Kirkstone Pass.

At the foot of the pass, a long, steep road near Ambleside, in Westmorland, they came upon a lone figure trudging up the hill. When they drew closer, they found the hiker was a wee Scout, all but lost under a huge rucksack which was packed to bursting point.

Like the Good Samaritan, when he saw the laddie, Mr Lewis had compassion on him, and pulled up.

" That's a big climb ahead of you, son," he said. " Can we give you a lift up the hill ?"

The Scout smiled and saluted. " Thank you, sir," he said. " But I'm on my honour to walk the distance." And with that he turned and marched resolutely on towards the top of the pass.

Oh, I know that, for many, honour is a word that's a bit old-fashioned these days. But to Mr Lewis—and, I may add, to me—the shining idealism of that young lad was a parable that is not only humbling but challenging.

TUESDAY—APRIL 21.

DID you hear about the somewhat exasperated little girl who confided in a friend ?

" Well," she sighed, " I suppose I shall have to go to Auntie's for tea, but she'll talk of nothing else except church and the Bible, and she's so awfully good that the only time I ever want to be bad is when I'm in her house."

Very naughty of her, I suppose, but very honest—and haven't we all awkward saints just like Auntie ?

WEDNESDAY—APRIL 22.

YOU think you cannot do it,
Quite sure you can't keep on.
You're tired out—you know it ;
All hope and cheer are gone.
Chin up ! With courage plod and plan !
Think you can do it—AND YOU CAN.

THURSDAY—APRIL 23.

HOW often the simplest thing can change our lives.

One day a boy of his own age spoke to Willie Swan in a street in Aberdeen. " Will ye come to the B.B. tonight ?" he asked.

" Why ?" countered Willie, who had never set eyes on the lad before.

" I've to get a recruit," said the lad perkily.

Well, Willie thought about it, and he did join the B.B. that night—and for the next 50 years he never ceased to be grateful to the still unknown lad who put the idea in his mind.

For the wonderful thing is, the B.B. became the great call to service in Willie's life. He was a wee shopkeeper. He never possessed many of the world's goods. But in his lifelong devotion to the work of the Brigade few men have become more richly endowed with friendship. Indeed, when he died, at the age of 62, I'm told a funeral service has rarely been more crowded, with people from every walk of life in Aberdeen.

Later Willie's ashes were taken to Deeside. And there, in a field of ripe corn where Willie's tented shop always stood at B.B. camps, they were scattered to the wind. Surely a fitting tribute to a man who in his life had sown so much good in the field of youth.

A CLEAN WIND BLOWING

Oh, what is like a clean north wind
To dry your washing white?
Or like a breeze from off the sea
To put your cares to flight?

DAVID HOPE

CHANGE

Eternal battle's fought between
The seeking sea and downland green.
When another age has gone
And other watchers look upon
A different scene, I hope they'll say
" How lovely !" as I here, today.

DAVID HOPE

I WAS down at the river the other day. A strong tide was running. The wind was inshore, so that it looked almost as if the river had gone into reverse! Running up with the tide came masses of driftwood, empty boxes, railway sleepers, refuse from ships—enough fuel, if it was gathered together, to keep many homes snug.

Of course, most of us are well enough off these days not to need to go foraging for firewood. But as I thought back to the time when men stood on the banks with ropes and hooks, pulling the stuff ashore, glad to take it home and saw it up, I couldn't help feeling a little sorry that we have lost so many good old-fashioned habits of saving.

WHAT a rash of antique shops there is today! And what odd things, like those thrown out when Granny died, are now cleaned up and in the window at crazy prices! It intrigued me recently to see this notice in a shop window in a side street. ANTIQUES. BOUGHT & SOLD. REPAIRED. REPOLISHED & MANUFACTURED.

But how can an antique be manufactured? To me a thing is worth buying only if it is beautiful or useful. It can be lovely if it was made two hundred years ago, or even if it was made yesterday.

I suppose it's easy to blame the dealers, but doesn't the blame lie partly with those who pay sweetly for anything they think is fashionable?

IN the beginning God created the heaven and the earth.

MONDAY—APRIL 27.

I COMBINED business with pleasure a week or so ago. I had to do some travelling, and took the Lady of the House with me. We spent some hours in Yorkshire; and near Malton discovered an utterly charming village. The sun shone on Nunnington all the time we were there—peering into the river as we stood on the stone bridge, admiring the gracious house near the crossroads, delighting in the pretty cottage and colourful gardens and the magnificent views over a green and pleasant land, and exploring the little old church.

While I looked at the figure of a knight in armour, the Lady of the House picked up a Bible which had fallen on the floor of a pew. It opened of its own accord where a faded scrap of paper had these lines, obviously written by a very elderly person. I think the writing was done during the 1939 to 1945 War, but the prayer is as much needed today as ever :—

Grant us, Lord, through all these days of war, light in our darkness; faith that overcomes all doubt; courage that subdues all fear; hope that never fails, and the peace of those whose minds are stayed on Thee. Amen.

TUESDAY—APRIL 28.

A FRIEND was reading a book a short time ago, and was so impressed by a single sentence that he copied it out and sent it to me. The sentence comes from the first chapter of Charles Reade's novel "The Cloister and the Hearth," and I think we might bear it in mind:—

Not a day passes but men and women of no note do great deeds, speak great words, and suffer noble sorrows.

WEDNESDAY—APRIL 29.

WE'RE two old folk who cough and croak—
  We have a friend next door ;
We've warmth and food and memories,
  Do we need any more ?
And when our son comes home from sea,
We're thrilled to make THREE cups of tea !

THURSDAY—APRIL 30.

ON a cold afternoon Mrs McMillan, of Glasgow, was standing at a bus stop near her home with her little boy, Martin, in her arms.

As she waited, an old man turned on to the road from the nearby cemetery. His face was sad, and he looked cold. Mrs McMillan knew without asking that he had just come from visiting the grave of someone very dear to him — his wife, perhaps, or a son.

As the man drew level with her, her wee boy reached out, as children do, and touched his coat. The old man stopped.

" Hello, son," he said, and smiled. Martin, aged only 15 months, smiled back — then, leaning over in his mother's arms, he gave the pensioner a kiss on the cheek.

For a moment the old man was silent. Then he whispered, " God bless you, son." And, patting the child's hand, he turned to go. As he did so, Mrs McMillan saw the tears filling his eyes, and she herself felt a lump in her throat. She says that it was a moment she will remember for the rest of her life.

I am sure the unknown pensioner will, too — and I can't help feeling that, in their way, the innocence and simple trust of a little child are a challenge and a rebuke to us all.

MAY

LATE one night, Rev. William Macartney, of Berwick-on-Tweed, motored into Dublin to look for his holiday digs. Alas, it wasn't long before he was hopelessly lost — and it was 2.15 a.m.

He was wondering what on earth he could do when he came on a brightly-lit bus depot with maintenance men working on rows of parked buses.

Mr Macartney asked one of them how to get to Tritonville Road. The man was anxious to help but he didn't know. He turned to his friend Joe, but Joe didn't know either.

"Will ye just be after givin' us a minute, sorr," they said respectfully—and disappeared among the ranks of silent buses.

Soon they reappeared triumphantly and pointed to a bus pulling out of the shed behind them. "That driver," they said, "knows Tritonville Road. Follow that bus, sorr, and he'll get you there." And he did. Right to the door.

Presidents get a motor cycle escort. But as Mr Macartney says, he must be the first-ever visitor to be escorted by a double-decker bus!

EVERYBODY in Bedford Row knows Granny Shaw. They look in to see her. Granny left school at thirteen — over seventy years ago, so she isn't well-educated, hasn't any degrees, isn't an authority on anything, and has never made a platform speech in her life. But a neighbour declares —" There's just nobody can listen as nicely as Granny Shaw can."

SUNDAY—MAY 3.

BE strong and of good courage : be not afraid, neither be thou dismayed : for the Lord thy God is with thee, whithersoever thou goest.

MONDAY—MAY 4.

ONE Saturday night, Mrs Scanlon of Bedford, spent an evening out at a club — one of those places that's always busy on a Saturday night, with every table packed, drinks being served, dancing, and a small stage show.

Suddenly, as everyone was laughing at the jokes of two comedians who held the stage, the door of the club opened and in walked a boy and a girl from the Salvation Army. They had come to sell the " War Cry "—but, as soon as they were spotted, one of the entertainers began to play " The Old Rugged Cross."

Then he asked the two young folk to come up to the stage and sing it. If they did, he said he would take round their papers and collecting box.

Without hesitation, the youngsters took their places on the stage, to loud cheers and clapping. As the applause died away the young man stepped forward and in a firm, clear voice said, " We aren't going to sing this to entertain you. We are singing it because we believe in what it says—and we know that the only way you can be truly happy is to believe in its message, too."

It was, in its way, a kind of rebuke. The audience fell silent, and, as the young Salvationists' song rang out, you could have heard a pin drop.

Need I add that their collecting tin was overflowing when they left—or that of all the memories Mrs Scanlon took home that night, this was the brightest ?

TUESDAY—MAY 5.

AT every chance at meal-time George would lean across the table to make a face at Tony when their mother was not looking. Then he would say "Boo!" The baby was frightened. Young George was jealous of his baby brother Tony, as the previous baby is sometimes apt to be. But one day, when he was about eleven months old, Tony made a face just as ugly at his older brother and said, "Boo!" firmly in return. Parents and children, all burst out laughing. Now the two youngest, both a little older, are firm friends.

If we have the courage to face up to the things which frighten us we may possibly find that they are quite harmless—maybe even friends.

WEDNESDAY—MAY 6.

*H*E'S made his pile. He's famous now,
 A big success is he,
But secrets doubts are his—he's not
 The man he meant to be.
And, oh, such lovely thoughts he had
 When, years ago, he was a lad.

THURSDAY—MAY 7.

I CAME across this reflection in a magazine. It is by H. L. Wayland, who remarks whimsically—
Last week I saw a man who has not made a mistake for four thousand years. He is a mummy in the British Museum.

It is a way of saying that only dead people never make mistakes, a way of reminding us that if you are alive and kicking and doing things, you're bound to make mistakes. Having made them, however, the big thing is not to make them again.

THE FRIENDSHIP BOOK

ALL that he had was a scrap of paper with her telephone number, and now it was lost. Indeed the young man looked completely lost himself, as, in halting English, he told me that he hailed from Madrid, in Spain. He was visiting Britain to see " a young lady " and now, he said, almost in tears, he had lost the only clue.

As aliens have to register with the police, I guessed that the police might know about her. So I directed him to the Central Police Station and last saw him striding off purposefully in that direction. Such is the determination of youth and young love that it will cross a country or a whole Continent, and without knowing the language it is still prepared to scour a big foreign city. I'm sure he found her!

THESE days, when we hear so much discussion about church unity, you might be interested in this story told by Dr Wilfred Grenfell, author of the book " Labrador Doctor."

One day in Labrador he had to amputate a woman's leg. She was a Roman Catholic. While on furlough in the U.S.A., the good doctor, speaking in a Congregational church, told of this woman's plight, and said if anybody had a spare wooden leg, he would be happy to accept it. Somebody had—a Methodist, who explained that her Presbyterian husband had died, and left his wooden leg in her keeping.

Dr Grenfell took the wooden leg back to Labrador. So he, an Episcopalian, fitted the Roman Catholic woman with a Presbyterian leg given by a Methodist widow in a Congregational church. And the woman walked!

SUNDAY—MAY 10.

THE secret things belong unto the Lord our God.

MONDAY—MAY 11.

AN old Scottish story tells of a mason in a Berwickshire village.

A passer-by found the old craftsman chiselling an unusually elaborate epitaph on a tombstone, and commented—"The lettering is excellent; and the man you are commemorating seems to have been little less than a saint."

The mason nodded. "Aye," he agreed, "the lettering's fine, though I say it mysel'; but the words are no' just what he was, but what he should ha'e been."

I don't suppose it matters a bit to you or me what is written on our tombstones. But I hope no-one has to make it up.

TUESDAY—MAY 12.

MRS SHARON took us proudly all through the clean "maternity ward" in the pig farm, where all the little piglets are born. Mrs Sharon knows every sow by name and they know her, responding to her voice. But this morning, because we were being taken round, one worthy matron was not allowed out for her usual walk.

And was she in the sulks! She turned her back on everyone and ignored our proffered hands. Later, said Mrs Sharon, she would allow this disgruntled lady out for her customary walk.

They say animals have no intelligence or reasoning power; but I do not agree, for here was this mother-to-be making it plain that she did not approve of the change from the normal custom!

BY THE WAY

A chap from town, he told us once,
That nothing happens here.
I wonder what he thinks we get
To talk about all year!

DAVID HOPE

THE BOWLER'S CREED

When worries are oppressing
And far-off seem my goals,
Give me a sunny afternoon,
A friendly game of bowls.

Pills may soothe your worries,
But we true bowlers think
We find a better medicine
As we battle on the rink.

DAVID HOPE

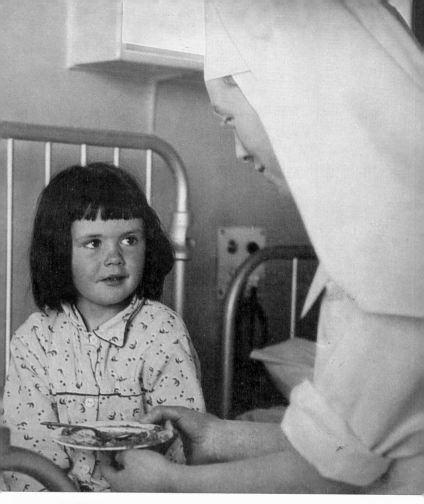

CARING

Bless hands that heal,
And hearts that feel,
And may they find
The peace of mind,
That they to others give.

DAVID HOPE

WEDNESDAY—MAY 13.

A HOUSE can scarcely be a home
Without a woman in it.
She is its life, its light, its joy,
In every single minute.
A house a heaven can become
If there's a patient, loving Mum!

THURSDAY—MAY 14.

I HAVE been privileged to hear of many tender farewells, but I think that this is one of the loveliest.

It is a story that began in 1954, when a young couple from Paisley, Frank and Anne Robertson, emigrated to Canada.

Frank went to work as an engineer, and Anne, a fine singer, found a job in broadcasting.

Then, when things were going so well, Frank fell seriously ill. Anne was called to the hospital where he lay, and she saw there was not much time left. She had so much she wanted to say to him in those precious last moments, but somehow she knew that words alone could never fully express what she felt. So, taking his hand in hers, she began to sing the song he loved above all others, and which spoke so eloquently of what was in her heart, " My Love Is Like A Red, Red Rose."

Her voice softly echoed through the hushed ward—

But fare thee weel, my only love,
So deep in love am I,
And I will love thee still, my dear,
Till a' the seas gang dry . . .

A few moments later, it was all over. But who can doubt that those last minutes of Frank's life were truly blessed.

FRIDAY—MAY 15.

THIS story was told by Rev. Stanley Pritchard, of Glasgow. It is about two elderly, unmarried sisters who lived together in the old family home, a fine house in the best part of the town. They were well known by all in the neighbourhood and those who visited them were received with old-world courtesy in the beautifully-furnished drawing-room.

Then one of the old sisters fell ill, and was taken to hospital. There, to the amazement of her doctors, it was found she wasn't suffering from an illness, but from under-nourishment.

Bit by bit, the real story emerged. The money they had been left had all gone. Over the years they had sold every stick of furniture except in the hall and drawing-room. They spent every penny they had on keeping up appearances, and lived on bread and margarine. Indeed, the "well-off" sisters were poorer than the poorest family in the poorest part of the city.

It is a tragic story, and it is surely a warning to us all that things are not always what they seem.

SATURDAY—MAY 16.

LORD BYRON, a poet and one of our most penetrating thinkers, once said profoundly—*Always laugh when you can. Merriment is a philosophy not well understood. It is the sunny side of existence.*

Whatever the psychologists may say, the fact is that anybody with a cheerful disposition, even if he or she has no end of trouble, comes through life with flying colours—and a lot of friends.

SUNDAY—MAY 17.

A LIVING dog is better than a dead lion.

THE FRIENDSHIP BOOK

MONDAY—MAY 18.

I CAME across this parable in Dr Albert Schweitzer's " Reverence For Life."

A flock of wild geese had settled to rest on a pond. One of the flock was captured by a gardener who clipped its wings before releasing it. When the geese started to resume their flight, this one tried frantically, but vainly, to lift itself into the air. The others, observing his struggles, flew about trying to encourage him; but it was no use.

Thereupon, the entire flock settled back on the pond and waited, even though the urge to go was strong within them. For several days they waited until the damaged feathers had grown sufficiently to permit the goose to fly.

This display of loyalty and self sacrifice touched the gardener's conscience, and when the geese finally all rose together and resumed their long flight, he watched them, relieved and glad.

TUESDAY—MAY 19.

AN English student was studying at one of the Scottish Divinity Halls. By way of cutting his teeth he had taken a trip to the Shetlands to help in an evangelistic campaign. As he went from door to door he found that his English accent carried certain inbuilt disadvantages.

The door would open cautiously to his knocking. Where was he from? England? (The situation was not much improved). But his father hailed from the North, Caithness in fact. (Well, that was better). The door would open wider. What about his mother? As a matter of fact, she was born and brought up in the Shetlands! Well, now, that was entirely different! Why didn't you say that at first? Come away in. The kettle is on the boil.

WEDNESDAY—MAY 20.

YOU cannot face another day?
  You're tired, sad and done?
You've lost all hope? Now life for you
  Has neither thrill nor fun?
Though cherished dreams of mine are gone,
I bid you, friend, keep on, keep on!

THURSDAY—MAY 21.

I'D like to pass on to you some lines which came to me from Mrs Ivy Johnstone, of Glasgow. She tells me she wrote them one day while sitting in her garden.

She'd just been reading about all the strikes and go-slows when a thought struck her. What on earth would happen, she wondered, if the things of Nature should decide to follow the ways of man?

Suppose the lovely rosebud should drop its dainty head, and say, " I'll spend each Sunday, shut tight in my rose bed."

Suppose the singing blackbird should close its orange beak, from Friday until Monday, and start a five-day week.

Suppose the sun stopped shining for just one single day; with twenty-four hours' darkness, how should we find our way?

Suppose the friendly milking cow walked through the cowshed door, and said, " You've had enough from me. I'm stopping work at four."

The more you pick the rosebuds, the more you'll see them grow; a blackbird's always singing, it's the happiest life they know.

So men should follow Nature, and learn to play their part, with smiles and songs and happy faith, and a willing hand and heart.

FRIDAY—MAY 22.

IN order to remind himself of something he might forget Francis Gay will occasionally tie a knot in the corner of his handkerchief; then as often as not when he pulls it out of his pocket he cannot remember why he ever tied it! Just so, Sir Walter Scott describes how in his day they would " lay in a leaf." They would turn in the corner of an appropriate page in the Bible to remind them of a certain passage. But it's not much use doing that if we are to forget why we did it in the first place!

SATURDAY—MAY 23.

THE Rev. David Phillips, of Bishopbriggs, told me this story about something that happened at one of the first weddings he ever conducted.

The bridegroom's name was John MacDonald. After the young couple had been pronounced man and wife, Mr Phillips turned to the 'groom and said, " Now you may kiss Mrs MacDonald." The congregation looked on with happy smiles—but their smiles soon broadened into grins of amusement.

To everyone's astonishment, the bridegroom, overcome with confusion, no doubt, left his bride's side, went over to the front pew—and kissed his mother! Of course, his new wife took it in good part and, tugging him gently by the arm, reminded him, " I'm Mrs MacDonald, too, now!"

Needless to say, it was the last time Mr Phillips ever invited the 'groom to kiss the bride during the wedding ceremony!

SUNDAY—MAY 24.

THE wages of sin is death.

THE FRIENDSHIP BOOK

LISTENING to a religious programme on the radio one morning we were delighted to hear a glorious rendition of this hymn—

O perfect Love, all human thought transcending,
Lowly we kneel in prayer before Thy throne,
That theirs may be the love which knows no ending,
Whom Thou for evermore dost join in one.

I'm sure the Lady of the House was misty-eyed as we listened—and waited for the announcer to tell why the beautiful wedding hymn had come to us out of the blue. But all he said was that it had been requested by a listener for an anniversary.

So we don't know who are the happy husband and wife who inspired such a lovely anniversary of their wedding morn. But, I would like to thank them for letting us share their joy.

I REMEMBER an elderly joiner doing a little thing in the house for me years ago; and I cannot forget the smile he gave me as he quoted what he called " the joiner's golden rule—measure twice before you saw once." There's wisdom for you.

And is it not the same at all times and in all things? When you get the sudden urge, think again before you do it!

WHEN sad your heart, and no birds sing,
When you in silence weep,
How dark each day—your lonely way
How long, how drear, how steep.
Yet all who hide their sorrows find
The world is really very kind.

THE FRIENDSHIP BOOK

THURSDAY—MAY 28.

ONE summer day, Mr and Mrs Blundell, of Liverpool, decided on the spur of the moment to spend a few days visiting Loch Lomond and The Trossachs. They'd planned nothing, but they knew they could always stay with relatives in Irvine for a couple of nights.

So you can imagine their disappointment when they arrived at the house in Irvine, at 8.15 one night and found no one at home. When they inquired next door, Mr and Mrs McPherson told them their relatives were away on holiday.

But what do you think? Without hesitating a moment, Mr and Mrs McPherson invited them in and gave them a lovely tea. Not only that, they offered them their own bed for as long as they wanted to stay. It was a wonderful gesture, and the result was that the Blundells' holiday in Irvine lasted for a week instead of just two nights!

Now the remarkable thing about all this is that Mr and Mrs McPherson had never met Mr and Mrs Blundell before. Yet, by the time the week came to an end, they were old friends, and though Mr and Mrs Blundell took many happy memories home with them, they left a bit of their hearts behind in Irvine.

FRIDAY—MAY 29.

IT may take less bravery than we think:—If, say, a man tackles a fire when he knows that if he doesn't get it out, he and his mates will blow up anyway.

Joan of Arc, facing the stake, had only to say that the voices she heard were devils and not angels. Then she might have gone free. Isn't that the stuff of real courage?

SATURDAY—MAY 30.

ONE wild night, a young mother sat nursing her baby in her home in Chryston, Glasgow.

It was nearly 3 a.m. Her child had a fever and would not be comforted. Her husband was away from home, and the poor woman was desperately wondering what to do. Then came a knock at the door—and there, to her amazement, stood her doctor, Dr John Jamieson. What had brought him? Well, apparently, whenever he was called out during the night and saw a light in the home of any of his patients, he stopped, to make sure all was well.

Usually he wasn't needed—but sometimes his call seemed almost providential. Before he left the child was sleeping peacefully and its mother knew that nothing was seriously wrong.

That, I am told, was typical not only of Dr John, but also of his brother, Dr George Jamieson. Together they looked after the folk of Chryston and Moodiesburn for more than 40 years.

Then, some years ago, Dr George died. Though Dr John carried on bravely, his brother's death had told heavily on him. Yet even when he knew he was ill himself, he kept going, until he too, died, still in his early 60's.

The two good doctors of Chryston were paid many fine tributes, but perhaps the tribute that would have made them happiest is that the great tradition they began is being carried on—for Dr John's son and Dr George's son and daughter have taken their places.

May I say they could not have two finer examples to follow?

SUNDAY—MAY 31.

IT is more blessed to give than to receive.

THE CORE OF THINGS

As at the core of the hurricane,
The great winds cease,
So by the river's endless thunder,
The heart finds peace.

DAVID HOPE

HOURS OF EASE

A grassy place, a little breeze,
The sunshine gently streaming:
It's blossom-time again and what
A lovely day for dreaming!

DAVID HOPE

JUNE

MONDAY—JUNE 1.

DON'T don't.

There is too much don't being done. What we need is fewer don'ts and a lot more do's.

This is addressed especially to Mum. It is easier to say to Jimmy: " Don't tease the cat," than to say: " Do help me polish the spoons."

But you can't make Jim a busy, cheery, helpful, contented laddie by telling him what not to do. Channel his strength and interest in a positive way —suggest good things he can do or try to do.

If you have a bairn growing up under your roof, help him along, guide him forward, take his arm, so to speak, and walk with him, at his speed, into a world of doing good. You will never regret it.

TUESDAY—JUNE 2.

I REMEMBER it every second of June.

A young girl asked us all to pray for her on that June day in 1953. Her voice went into millions of homes and touched millions of hearts, for the girl was our Queen, and it was her Coronation Day.

" I want to ask you all," she said, " whatever your religion may be, to pray for me—to pray that God may give me wisdom and strength to carry out the solemn promise I shall be making, and that I may faithfully serve Him and you, all the days of my life."

Today is the seventeenth anniversary of Coronation Day. The glitter and pomp of the great day have long since faded. But one thing can never fade—the Queen's example of her faith in the power of prayer.

That is why, every second of June, I give thanks we are blessed with such a gracious and God-fearing woman as our Queen.

WEDNESDAY—JUNE 3.

A LITTLE work, a little fun,
　　And then our little day is done.
But he who sings a merry song
And gladly helps a friend along,
His life has worth and pleasure in it—
He uses every sparkling minute !

THURSDAY—JUNE 4.

THIS story warmed my heart, just as I'm sure it will warm yours.

One day during the week, old Mrs Beckett toddled through the gates of Crookston Eventide Home in Glasgow and made her way to the bus stop. She was off on a visit to her son and daughter-in-law. in Cardonald, and when the No. 23 bus came along she climbed on carefully.

" I'm awfully slow," she said to the cheery bus conductor. But he just smiled. " You take your time, Granny," he replied. " We can always wait for old folk." Mrs Beckett nodded. " Well," she announced, with understandable pride, " It's my birthday today and I'm 89."

The bus conductor was thrilled and he told her so. But he did more. When the bus pulled up a little later, he had a quick word with the driver, and disappeared into a sweetie shop.

Then he swung himself back aboard his bus, marched up to Granny Beckett's seat and, with a bow and a flourish, presented her with his compliments—and a half-pound box of chocolates.

Oh, Mrs Beckett's family made a great fuss of her later on, and there were gifts and cards galore. But, between you and me, I doubt if any of them delighted her more than the surprise she got from Sir Galahad on the 23 bus !

THE FRIENDSHIP BOOK

<u>FRIDAY—JUNE 5.</u>

HERE'S a lovely story that came to light when an American lawyer, Mr George Ray, visited his friends, Mr and Mrs Macartney, in Berwickshire.

They had much to talk about, of course, and sat chatting until late. Then, just before they all went to bed, Mr Macartney asked Mr Ray what his family in America would be doing. As you know, it's never the same hour there as it is here.

But Mr Ray didn't look at his wrist-watch. Instead, he reached into his waistcoat pocket and brought out another watch. " Nearly seven o'clock," he said, adding that his wife would be calling his grandchildren to come in for supper.

Then he explained that when he is far from home, he carries two watches. The one on his wrist tells the time in the country he is visiting. The other, he keeps at the time it would be if he were back home in Vermont. So, wherever he may be, he can glance at his pocket watch, and know pretty well what his family is doing at that moment.

In a way, it helps to keep him close to them, even though he is thousands of miles from home.

As I say—isn't this a lovely story ?

<u>SATURDAY—JUNE 6.</u>

THE other morning on my way across the moor I noticed a wonderful spider's web, stretching over the long grass and heather, a perfect piece of gossamer. You could be sure it was going to be a hot and sunny day. These gentlemen, who make such webs, have not the slightest intention of doing this work on a day when it is going to be wasted. TV weather forecasts may be getting more accurate all the time, but it will be a long time ere they are as accurate as these, from the humble spider.

THE FRIENDSHIP BOOK

SUNDAY—JUNE 7.

SPEAK, Lord ; for Thy servant heareth.

MONDAY—JUNE 8.

IF ever you feel a bit glum early in the day, you might do worse than quote these lines—and then do what they suggest—

Take a moment or two to look upward
When the morning is newly begun;
Looking down you will merely see shadows—
Looking up you will see the bright sun !

TUESDAY—JUNE 9.

ON my way home about 5.30 the other afternoon a young gentleman halted me with the words : " Hello, Mr Gay. I'm going to marry your wife."

This struck me as interesting. " Indeed," I murmured. " Why ?"

" Because she has a kind face, and is very jolly."

I nodded. It seemed to me a quite sensible reason. " And does she want to marry *you* ?" I asked.

" Oh, yes. She says I'm super. But it won't be just yet."

Realising there was nothing I could do about the matter, I considered the young gentleman, who was sitting on a wall, dangling his legs. " And what," I inquired, " are you doing in the meantime ?"

The young gentleman thought. " If I had some money," he mused, " I'd lick a lolly."

So I gave him enough money for a lolly, and he ran off to the shop at the corner, hoping it would still be open. Then I went indoors, and the Lady of the House gave me a hug. I think we are likely to continue living together, at any rate till the little boy two doors away has finished his lolly.

THE FRIENDSHIP BOOK

WEDNESDAY—JUNE 10.

WHAT if the summer sky is blue
If winter's in your heart?
How can you keep on day by day,
How CAN you play your part?
If faith and courage have not gone
You'll find you can keep plodding on!

THURSDAY—JUNE 11.

MRS B. KYLE is head teacher at Roxburgh Primary School, Kelso.

One day she took 30 of her children on an outing to Edinburgh Zoo. They were driving along without a care in the world when their bus driver suddenly jammed on his brakes. A stranger had dashed into the road and signalled the driver to stop. A moment later, he was telling Mrs Kyle he had a message for them.

Dear me, thought Mrs K. What on earth had happened? She was mystified, but not for long.

For the stranger disappeared into a nearby shop —and came out again carrying an enormous box of sweets and chocolate which he handed to Mrs Kyle. Bless my soul, there was enough in the box for a treat for everyone, including the driver (and, I'm told, enough left over for another handout at school play-time next day!)

It turned out that the stranger had been driving behind the bus and had been taken by the children waving happily to him.

So, he overtook the bus and drove ahead to the first sweetie shop to buy them all a treat. Indeed, he bought so many sweets he'd to dash out of the shop and stop the bus going past until the sweets were all packed in a box. Hence the dramatic incident of the mystery man who stopped the bus!

FRIDAY—JUNE 12.

I HAVE been watching little Amanda (3½) lying on a bathtowel, face-down in the sun, on the balcony of her parents' flat. She is quite exhausted with playing and paddling on the beach. Now she sleeps in her tiny bikini; but the sun is really far too hot for her young skin. Already her mother has crept out and placed a wickerwork chair above her, and now her father has put a rug across it so that only a few of the hot rays can reach her. While we have lunch Amanda sleeps on, undisturbed.

Isn't it true that not one of us knows what unseen hands of love did for us when we were too young to care for ourselves? Or what unknown forces for good shielded us when unwittingly we had placed ourselves in danger?

SATURDAY—JUNE 13.

IN 1960 a religious organisation was holding a mission in the island of Mull. A man who had scorned faith for years was deeply moved by a verse in the Bible which had been read to him. Suddenly he seemed to lose his bitterness and uncertainty. He declared his belief, and sang because only a hymn could express the new joy he felt.

Next morning, however, one of the mission workers met the new convert, who looked anything but happy. " Well," she asked, " what gave you the joy and assurance you had last night?"

" It was that verse you quoted," said the man.

" I see," was the reply. " And isn't that verse in the Bible this morning?"

SUNDAY—JUNE 14.

THOU shalt love thy neighbour as thyself.

THE FRIENDSHIP BOOK

MONDAY—JUNE 15.

A YOUNG mother boarded a crowded bus with a baby and two big parcels in her arms.

As she edged up the bus, she deposited her child in the lap of a clergyman who was seated near the front. He looked up at her with a smile. " I'm often told I've a grand way with children," he said, " but how did you know to pick on me ?"

The young woman looked at him innocently. " Oh," she replied, " you have such a kind face— and besides, you're the only passenger wearing a raincoat . . . !"

TUESDAY—JUNE 16.

WALKING along in the sunshine the other morning I met a transport driver I have known for more than twenty years as Charlie. The Lady of the House and I always refer to him as Cheerful Charlie because he has a smiling face and a genial manner. " Hello," I said. " On holiday ?"

" Not really," was the reply, the tone of voice anything but cheerful.

" Something wrong ?"

He nodded. " It's my wife. I've had to take special leave. She's had a stroke. Paralysed down the left side. Doctor says it may be due partly to shock— you maybe didn't know her sister died a fortnight ago. So I'm seeing to things till our daughter comes over for a while. And my wife's only forty-six."

We stood there mutely in the bright light of day, conscious, acutely so, that life has deep shadows. And I said . . .

But what *could* I say ? What could friend or minister or scholar say ? If I tell you what I said, will it not sound feeble, inadequate, trite, utterly worthless ?

I said: " I'm sorry, Charlie."

WEDNESDAY—JUNE 17.

SOME folk would rather run a mile—
A mile or even two—
Than say a word of cheer or praise,
It's what they dare not do.
A pity, since by doing it
They'd warm their own hearts just a bit!

THURSDAY—JUNE 18.

HERE'S a story to make you smile!

The cat at the Bank Pit, New Cumnock, had five kittens, and to the surprise of the miners, one of them was pure white. The men thought they'd never seen such a bonnie kitten, so they decided to adopt it.

Of course, before long the kitten's white fur was anything but white. What else could you expect down a coal mine, after all? So the miners called her " Sooty "—and soon she was a firm favourite.

Then one day five of the miners sat having their " piece " and sharing it, as usual, with Sooty. " You know," they said to each other, " that's a real bonnie cat. She'd win a prize anywhere."

Well, there was a big cat show in Glasgow soon, so why not enter Sooty? Sooty was taken home, given two baths, brushed and combed, and off she went in a basket to the show.

I don't expect any of the miners really thought Sooty had a chance of winning—but, by jove, she fairly showed them. She won not only one prize, but three and, to their delight, was judged the best cat in the show!

Now Sooty's hour of glory is past. She is back underground again, happily hunting mice along the dark tunnels. But to the miners she'll always be the pride of the pit.

FRIDAY—JUNE 19.

WHEN things perplex you, remember Christopher Columbus !

You see, when Columbus set out on his famous voyage of discovery, he didn't know *where he was going*. When he arrived on the strange shores of America, he didn't even know *where he was*. When he got back, he didn't even know *where he'd been*.

And yet he knew beyond a shadow of doubt that he had found a great, new world.

SATURDAY—JUNE 20.

MR FRANK REYNOLDS, of Essex, wrote to tell me about a friend of his, Jim Steward, who had some neighbours in for a game of bridge.

Suddenly the door opened, and in walked Jim's two small children, one behind the other, without a stitch of clothing on. Solemnly, and looking straight ahead, they marched round the table and out the door.

Everyone was too astonished to say a word. But as soon as the bairns had gone upstairs, their mother went after them.

She found them screaming with laughter.

" Mummy," they shouted, " we've been having great fun. We found a jar of vanishing cream on your dressing table, and we wiped it all over us, and we went downstairs and walked all around the room— AND NOBODY SAW US !"

SUNDAY—JUNE 21.

BEHOLD, I stand at the door and knock : if any man hear my voice and open the door, I will come in to him, and will sup with him, and he with me.

THE FRIENDSHIP BOOK

MONDAY—JUNE 22.

THE house is hung with her pictures. My friend's
name is Gertrude and her age is 75; but I
always call her "Grandma Moses" after the
American lady who took up painting in old age—
far past 75—and astonishingly achieved world fame.

Getrude is a widow and she, too, began to paint
in water colours and then in oils when past the age
of 70. I doubt if her painting will ever be as famous
as that of the original Grandma Moses. For me,
however, it has a certain fascination, for she always
paints like a young child, setting down exactly what
she sees. The trouble for so many is that we are so
full of prejudices that we are never able, even in
writing a letter or telling a story, to describe
exactly what took place. But the charm of children
of whom it was said, " Of such is the kingdom of
heaven " need not be lost, even in old age.

TUESDAY—JUNE 23.

ONE glorious afternoon recently a woman said
good-bye to her husband in hospital, and
hurried from the ward so as not to be late when she
arrived at the infant school her son attends. But what
a turmoil was in her heart—after his operation, her
husband had had a relapse and was even then in an
oxygen tent, a very sick man.

Harassed and anxious, the young wife met her
wee boy coming out of school. His face was all
smiles, his eyes bright. He took her hand and said,
" Look happy, Mummy. I'm taking you home !"

Next day, when she was told her husband had
died, that woman found comfort and even some
happiness in the challenging thought that her boy—
his boy—would take her hand as she walked in the
dark valley on a sunny day.

WEDNESDAY—JUNE 24.

*I*N *my wheeled chair I get a lot*
  Of pleasure from my garden plot,
Aubretia and nasturtiums glow—
  I love to watch such sweetness grow.
My garden is a daily thrill—
  It rests upon the window-sill.

THURSDAY—JUNE 25.

MRS AINSWORTH, of Bolton, spent a holiday in Wales a few years ago. Walking along the promenade at Prestatyn, she and her daughter sat down on a bench for a rest, and were joined by a stranger, a middle-aged woman.

Together they watched some children playing. The woman called them all to her and, after asking their names, gave them each a shilling for sweets and ice-cream. Then, turning to Mrs Ainsworth, she said how much she loved children.

She went on to say her husband had died, she had never been blessed with a family, and she was now alone. She had come away by herself for a few days because of a grave decision she'd to make.

It seems she had suffered for years from an illness which was steadily getting worse. Now she had been told she could have an operation, but there was only a 50-50 chance of success.

How difficult it must have been for her . . . to be alone with such a terrible decision on her mind. Mrs Ainsworth tried to help as much as she could, and when at length they parted, the woman said she had decided to risk the operation. If it wasn't a success, she hoped she might not wake from it.

So they parted, but Mrs Ainsworth still remembers that brave and lonely woman she met on a park bench in Wales.

FRIDAY—JUNE 26.

ONE Friday three widows from Dundee set out for a car run to Dunkeld.

It was a perfect summer day. At Dunkeld they found a quiet spot on the river bank for their picnic, and it was so warm they were able to sit out until nearly eight o'clock. They will never forget the beauty of that scene. The trees on the opposite bank, so green and fresh . . . trout jumping in the the clear water . . . and, above all, the peacefulness.

Then, just as they were about to leave, they heard the bells of the old cathedral pealing out the favourite tune of Psalm 23, " Crimond." The three women stood spellbound, for somehow it couldn't have been more appropriate—the green fields around them . . . the quiet waters . . . aye, and their restored souls, too.

I am told that every day the carillon of Dunkeld Cathedral chimes out three times—at eight in the morning, with the Old Hundredth; at noon, with " I To The Hills Will Lift Mine Eyes "; and every evening at eight, " Crimond," drifting out over the countryside. Isn't it a lovely tradition ?

SATURDAY—JUNE 27.

THE class was a large one, made up of girls about eight or nine years of age. As they practised hard at their writing, teacher was walking up and down between the desks watching them closely. One little girl was making such heavy weather of the job and muttering away to herself that she paid no attention to the approaching footsteps. Leaning over the desk to examine this prodigy's handwriting, teacher could not but overhear what was being said over and over again. " Oh !" she muttered softly, " I wish I was married and away out of here !"

THE FRIENDSHIP BOOK

SUNDAY—JUNE 28.

THE price of wisdom is above rubies.

MONDAY—JUNE 29.

AT the school sports I always like to watch the mile race. My attention is gripped, not by the crack runners battling it out at the front, but by the two at the tail who are competing strongly still, so as not to be last. They could so easily have dropped out and never been missed.

On the last day of the same week we may go along to the assembly hall to see the annual presentation of prizes. There's a great cheer—and rightly so—for the school dux, and nearly as big a cheer for the runner-up. But I notice even more the rows and rows of pupils who could have dodged off elsewhere on this last day of term, but come along just the same to give the winner a cheer.

TUESDAY—JUNE 30.

I SAT on the hillside the other morning, very quietly, but making good use of a fine pair of field glasses. After a time the birds became used to my being there and approached much nearer. Soon by watching carefully and continuing to keep still I was able to determine one or two varieties, not very common visitors to our island, or what they call migrants, only spotted by those who may be watching in the right places.

It was all very thrilling, with the sun beating down on me, and these rare and beautiful strangers coming so near. It made me think of an old text in the Bible : " Be still, and know that I am God." We seem to have lost much of the art of being still.

JULY

WHEN things don't go just as you'd like,
    You can begin to grouse,
Or fret or sulk, or cause a gloom
    To settle on the house.
But what's the use ? It does no good,
    It helps nobody through;
And if somebody's hurt at all,
    That somebody is you.
How happy all your folk will be
    If your depression they CAN'T see !

THURSDAY—JULY 2.

THE famous doctor, Tournier, had a patient—a girl—who suffered from a form of anaemia. After analysing her blood, he suggested to the district medical officer that she should be sent to a mountain sanatorium.

The M.O. agreed, but pointed out that his analysis of the patient's blood did not tally with Dr Tournier's. The latter took a second sample and, to his astonishment, got a different blood count which indicated a great improvement in the girl's condition.

" Tell me," he said to her, " has anything important happened to you since my last visit ?"

" Yes," she replied. " After a long delay, I suddenly found I could forgive somebody against whom I had a grudge. I have felt very much better from that."

I suggest this is a story worth thinking about, for it seems that unkind thoughts and ill-will can affect a person's health. The Old Book puts it this way, " As a man thinketh in his heart, so is he."

FRIDAY—JULY 3.

MRS HANSON, of the Scottish Old Age Pensioners' Association, was out rattling her box one day, collecting for her old folk, when a boy of about eight stared at her and ventured to ask—"What are you collecting for, Missis?"

That was a fine chance for Mrs Hanson to tell him she was collecting to give a lot of grannies a day out. The small boy listened and turned to walk off without a word. But he was thinking. Suddenly he ran back. "I haven't got a granny," he said, "but here's threepence for yours." And into the box went three pennies for a very good cause!

SATURDAY—JULY 4.

IT'S quite a thrill to hear and see her laugh — so warm and hearty.

Yet she is bedfast. She hasn't been out of doors for fifteen years. Perhaps the most exciting thing that happens to her is somebody calling and sharing a bit of news, particularly good news.

One of the happiest souls living, she looks back to the days when she was up at half-past four on six mornings a week, walked five miles, rain or shine, to her job on a farm, trudged home five miles after a long and hard day's work. She has been poor for over ninety years, and happy nearly every minute of it because, she tells me, she doesn't like being miserable.

It just goes to show what you can do, and be, with next to nothing!

SUNDAY—JULY 5.

BLESSED are the peacemakers : for they shall be called the children of God.

MONDAY—JULY 6.

EVEN devout churchgoers—some of them, any-how—feel unable to sing, as the Psalmist urges them, simply because they just haven't a tuneful voice.

But a very understanding poet of our own day gives us these comforting lines:—

Praise the Lord in merry song,
Praise Him, praise Him all day long.
But what of me? I cannot sing—
I have no melody to bring.
Read The Word, oh joy of joys;
The Lord says: Make a joyful *noise!*

TUESDAY—JULY 7.

"AND what are you doing these days?" my friend, Mr George Gibb, of Paisley, asked an acquaintance.

"Oh," was the reply, "just killing time."

With a whimsical smile Mr Gibb replied, "I fancy you're wrong. Time's killing you!"

How true that is. Every minute you and I have one less minute to live.

It's a pity to kill time; a pity not to have some-thing to do worth doing. There are so many folk needing help, so many causes needing your support that it's a bit odd if you've time to kill time!

WEDNESDAY—JULY 8.

A LITTLE knock, a little pause,
A neighbour at your door.
A little news, exchange of views,
A bite and sup—no more.
Although you haven't been away,
Somehow you've had a holiday!

ON THE ROAD

With a bite to eat in your old rucksack
And the sunshine warm upon your back,
What's it matter the road you go
When the whole wide world is yours to know.

DAVID HOPE

IN PRAISE OF WEEDS

Marguerite and buttercup
The farmer can't abide;
He likes to see the barley wave
And never a weed beside.

Bless the farmer, bless the crop
But may man ne'er succeed
In banishing from off the earth
The lovely, useless weed!

DAVID HOPE

THE FRIENDSHIP BOOK

THE new stained glass window was duly installed in the parish church. That it ever came about was thanks largely to the aid of an American millionaire who was often holidaying in the district. But when the minister sent a cable inviting him to perform the unveiling, all that came back was a curt refusal. This was a great mystery, since the kindly American had clearly expressed his desire to be present. Indeed, the puzzle was only solved next summer when it became possible to talk things over and compare the cable that was sent with the one which actually arrived. As transmitted the cable included the clause — " THANKS LARGELY TO THE GENEROUS SUCCOUR FROM AMERICA." But what the millionaire received was this—" THANKS LARGELY TO THE GENEROUS SUCKER FROM AMERICA." It is nice to be able to report that diplomatic relations were then restored !

I HAVE received a small, yellow card — yellow with age — which used to be framed. It hung for years in the kitchen of a Victorian house in Edinburgh, and I am assured that at least three generations of housewives glanced at it many and many times. In a neat, round hand are just five words—BOTHER IT. DO IT FIRST.

Good advice in the kitchen, I think—and perhaps anywhere else. If there is anything unpleasant that must be done, if you hate paring potatoes or washing the step or cleaning the flues, don't think about it, don't postpone it, don't be miserable thinking about it . . . get it done.

And then enjoy doing the things you like.

SATURDAY—JULY 11.

ON a hill overlooking Greenock stands Gateside Prison for women.

In 1955 Miss Elizabeth Hobkirk took over as governor there, and when she stepped through the gates for the first time a sorry sight met her eyes. Round the prison chapel was a broad expanse of waste ground, with a few tired cabbages growing here and there, but little else.

Now Miss Hobkirk believes (as I do) that though prison is there for a purpose, it needn't be a place of gloom and depression. So, quietly, she set about transforming the wilderness into a garden. She began by working there herself and, one by one, the prisoners joined in until almost every one of the women was working beside her.

As the years passed, other corners were tackled. And now you could hardly believe it's the same old place.

When I paid a visit I saw rose beds ablaze with colour, herbaceous borders with every imaginable kind of flower blooming in them, rockeries and ramblers, all set amid wide green lawns, and making a perfect picture round the little, white-walled chapel. It is small wonder it's the pride and joy of all at Gateside.

But, in a way, it means even more. For surely it says to those who are sent there that a shadowed past can still have a sunny future. That, I believe, is the message of the garden of Gateside Prison.

SUNDAY—JULY 12.

WHO shall not fear Thee, O Lord, and glorify Thy name? for Thou only art holy : for all nations shall come and worship before Thee ; for Thy judgments are made manifest.

THE FRIENDSHIP BOOK

MONDAY—JULY 13.

HERE'S a tale a friend of mine loved to relate years ago. I doubt if it is true.

One summer evening, when dusk was deepened into twilight, my friend John and his wife were sitting in the Italian Gardens at Scarborough when a young man and a pretty girl sat on a seat below. The courting couple talked quietly and romantically, evidently unaware they were being overheard.

At last my friend's wife whispered—" We ought not to spy on them like this, John. Hadn't you better cough or something to warn them we're here? I'm sure he's going to propose."

John (so he used to say) muttered—" *Warn* him? Why should I? Nobody warned me when I proposed!"

TUESDAY—JULY 14.

IT'S an old army trick.

I tell it here because a Paisley mother actually put it into practice recently, with excellent results. You might call it—how to make friends.

The mother has two sons, aged 13 and 11. Normally they get on like a house on fire, but a few days ago they fell out, and though they didn't come to blows, they sulked and were most unpleasant to each other. So Mum gave each a duster and set them to polish the kitchen window.

Mad as mad, they reluctantly obeyed, grumbling under their breath as they began the chore. There they were, one on each side of the glass facing each other, polishing half-heartedly, furious inside, and glowering at each other. But it was no use; and in the end the two laddies couldn't finish the task for laughing !

So all's well.

WEDNESDAY—JULY 15.

IF things for you are all dead wrong,
If happiness takes wing,
You simply cannot dance for joy,
Or like a blackbird sing.
But you can somehow wear a grin,
Until your luck at last is in.

THURSDAY—JULY 16.

ON a fine summer morning I came upon two smiling youths standing by the side of the Great North Road.

They were borne down under enormous rucksacks, and before them was a placard which proclaimed they were German students, and would be grateful for a lift to Perth. Well, I pulled up and invited them to hop in.

Their names, I found, were Wolfgang and Joseph. They had been touring Scotland during their holidays, and had been thrilled by the grandeur of the Highlands and the friendliness of the folk they'd met. Soon they'd be back in their home town of Munster, where, they told me, they were studying English.

And then they asked me if I could help with a grammatical point which perplexed them.

"Certainly," I smiled confidently—whereupon the lads explained they had great difficulty in understanding whether they should say "I, too" or "Me, too." Could I tell them? Frankly, on the spur of the moment I hadn't a ready answer. So, to save my pride, I said simply that it all depended on the context in which it was used! I confess that long after I waved good-bye to the two happy wanderers at Perth, I was still wrestling with their poser.

FRIDAY—JULY 17.

I PAUSED, looked, and listened—and wondered.

I had overtaken two small boys who were walking slowly, deep in conversation. Then they stopped. "She said we had to share it," piped one laddie.

"Aye," the other agreed, "and share and share alike."

Obviously the moment of decision had come. A large apple rested on top of a wall. Both looked anxiously at each other. Then one of the boys said, "Go on. You cut. I'll choose."

What a marvellous way of ensuring that an apple is equally shared—one cuts, the other chooses. It's fair and quick. It gives the honest boy his reward—half an apple. It stops the dishonest boy cutting the apple unfairly.

It left me reflecting that perhaps this world could do with fewer conferences and arguments if only we had the simple techniques evolved by boys centuries ago.

SATURDAY—JULY 18.

I LIKE this story about Charles W. Eliot, late president of Harvard University, U.S.A.

During an educational conference one of the prominent speakers said, "Allow me to congratulate you on the miracles you have performed in this university. Since becoming president, sir, Harvard has become a wonderful storehouse of knowledge."

"That is indeed true," replied Eliot graciously, but with a whimsical smile. "I myself, however, can scarcely claim credit for it. It is simply that freshmen bring in so much knowledge and the seniors take so little out."

SUNDAY—JULY 19.

BE sure your sin will find you out.

MONDAY—JULY 20.

THE other evening the Lady of the House and I went for a little run into the country. It really was a pleasure to be alone, to stop here and there and admire the view, to travel slowly and comfortably in the evening light, and come to a halt for ten enriching minutes of silence.

It was after ten when I garaged the car. " Well," I remarked to the Lady of the House, " we can hardly say we have been on a big adventure."

My wife nodded. Then she said, " But it's nice sometimes to go nowhere and then come home."

Even now I'm not sure if that is utter rubbish or something very profound.

TUESDAY—JULY 21.

HAVE you heard the story of the young kirk elder and his newly-wed wife?

It was his turn for duty in church on the first Sunday after the honeymoon. His wife was at the service, too, of course, but as the sermon dragged on she became more and more concerned about the Sunday dinner she'd left cooking in the oven. Finally, in desperation, she scribbled a note on a piece of paper and handed it to another elder to pass on to her husband. He did.

But the husband, thinking the message was for the minister, quietly walked to the pulpit and handed it up to him. The minister halted in the midst of his sermon, unfolded the slip of paper, and was astonished to read—" Please go home and turn off the gas."

WEDNESDAY—JULY 22.

WHAT CAN we say to those who weep
For wife or husband dear?
How CAN we comfort or sustain
When loneliness they fear?
The utmost we can do perhaps,
Is share their bitter grief;
Our sympathy, though ill-expressed,
May help to bring relief.
A listening ear, a helping hand,
Can show we somehow UNDERSTAND.

THURSDAY—JULY 23.

CALL this a parable, if you like. Call it a sermon even, for in a way it is both of these.

Miss Rice, of St Annes, has arthritis and must walk with a stick. As she stepped forward to board a bus one day a young woman noticed the struggle she was having, helped her to a seat, and sat down beside her.

Gratefully Miss Rice turned to say " Thank you "—and as she did so, the young woman took a notebook from her handbag, wrote something down, and showed it to her. To her surprise, Miss Rice saw her young friend had written—" Isn't it a lovely day? I'm both deaf and dumb."

Before she could reply, the bus drew up at the young woman's stop—and, squeezing Miss Rice's hand, she smiled and jumped off with a cheery wave.

Miss Rice suffers from asthma as well as arthritis and things can sometimes be a bit of a trial for her. But, my goodness, seeing how one so young could meet life so happily with such handicaps, made her forget her own troubles and remember all her blessings.

FRIDAY—JULY 24.

A MOTHER of four has this recipe for a happy day. "It's the first hour-and-a-half that counts," says she. "If only I can get my man to work on time and in a good mood; if only I can keep my temper when the kids are exasperating, and all talk at once ; if only I can get Granny — who is still on the sick-list — washed and dressed and downstairs . . . and still have a smile, the rest of the day usually takes care of itself!"

SATURDAY—JULY 25.

DID you know it's 106 smiles from Newcastle to Edinburgh ? Yes, I mean *smiles*, not miles —and if you read on you'll see why. One day Mrs Margaret Harrison, of Newcastle, and some young Norwegian children who were staying with her, set off on a car run to Edinburgh.

On the way, the children were looking out of the back window of the car, smiling (as youngsters always do) at the following motorists. Alas, smile as they would, one grim-faced motor cyclist wouldn't smile back. So one of them took a piece of paper, wrote the word "SMILE" on it, and placed it on the back window. In a second or two the motor cyclist's expression changed to a friendly grin.

Well, that was only the beginning. On every trip that followed, the hours sped by as dour faces lit up at the youngsters' command !

What a marvellous way to make a long journey seem shorter—by turning the miles into smiles!

SUNDAY—JULY 26.

FATHER, into Thy hands I commend my spirit.

SUNNY DAYS

A look at this, a look at that,
A cup of tea, a little chat;
And that, I'm sure, is just the way
To make the most of holiday.

DAVID HOPE

MAKE BELIEVE

This train's the Golden Arrow,
The Flying Scot, the Brighton Belle.
It goes the way we'd go;
Our station — who can tell?

This train's a train of dreams —
I'd hate to be so old,
That I can't catch the gleams
That tincture youth with gold.

DAVID HOPE

THROUGH MEMORY'S EYE

Far above the clouds are flying,
Down the hill a breeze is sighing,
All as I remember, many years ago.
And if I climb no longer,
Still my love it beats the stronger,
And at heart I'm still the lad I used to know.

DAVID HOPE

MONDAY—JULY 27.

THE boy next door dragged his old bike out of the shed, to go for a run in the country. The back wheel wouldn't turn. His dad took one glance at the cycle and said three words—" Try some oil !"

The treatment worked, and off the boy went !

And you can use a " drop of oil " in the street, at your work, or in the home to prevent things going wrong. The " oil " may be a grin, a chuckle, a little hug for somebody who feels hurt, a word of praise or thanks, a small treat, or even not remarking the potatoes are under-done.

They're all such little things, but they make up the oil that keeps life's machinery running smoothly.

TUESDAY—JULY 28.

WE were in the garden recently, when the telephone rang.

I hurried indoors, raised the receiver, and heard a woman's voice, very excited, say—

" Darling, I've just heard about Nancy—thought I was never going to — it's a boy !"

A pause. Then—" Say, aren't you Jim ?"

" No," I replied. " But I'm thrilled all the same !"

So the stranger who had got the wrong number rang off . . . and I went into the garden to inform the Lady of the House it was a boy !

WEDNESDAY—JULY 29.

REMEMBER, if you cruise or snooze
Or drive a car or laze,
Those invalids and cripples who
Stay put on summer days.
And if you're tanned, and all goes fine,
Please drop the stay-at-homes a line.

THURSDAY—JULY 30.

WILLIE WILLIAMS was the son of a Welsh farmer and the brightest laddie in the school.

It was obvious Willie had it in him to go far in any profession. So he decided to study to become a doctor.

For a year or two all went well. Then one day, when young Willie was riding home from college, he saw a strange figure standing on a raised stone in a village churchyard speaking to those who had gathered round him. As he rode past, something the preacher said caught his attention, and he reined in his horse.

Little did he know it was to change his whole life—for it was that experience that made him give up all thought of becoming a doctor and decide instead to be a minister. For 50 years he travelled thousands of miles all over Wales, preaching the faith he had found in a country churchyard as a young man of 20.

He was, I am sure, thinking of himself when, not long after he began his mission, he wrote:—

Guide me, O Thou great Jehovah,
Pilgrim through this barren land;
I am weak, but Thou art mighty;
Hold me with Thy powerful hand . . .

Isn't it amazing that, but for a chance encounter, this splendid hymn with its thrilling message might never have been?

FRIDAY—JULY 31.

FOR those who are growing old, this thought may be not only a comfort, but a staff—

I find that with the passing years my pace is just a little slowed; I may not go so fast or far—but I see more along the road.

AUGUST

SATURDAY—AUGUST 1.

YOU can say, "Happy birthday." You can sing "Happy birthday."

But has anyone expressed the wish more charmingly than the granddaughter of Mrs Beadie, of Rutherglen, who sent these lines from Toronto?—

*Count not your age in years you live, but by the
   happiness you give,*
*The friends you make, the good you do, the con-
   fidence that's placed in you;*
*The little things that day by day bring cheer to others
   on life's way;*
*And count this birthday one more mile upon the
   Road of Things Worthwhile.*

SUNDAY—AUGUST 2.

THE hope of the righteous shall be gladness.

MONDAY—AUGUST 3.

WE were last to arrive in the hotel dining-room; most of the other guests were just leaving. After our meal we sat in the TV room before going to bed, but nobody spoke to us. We both felt they seemed to be a particularly unfriendly lot.

But next morning the sun was shining, everyone spoke to us at breakfast, and the hotel which had seemed dingy the night before was now bright and attractive. Then we realised that the fault had been in ourselves. We had both been tired after a long drive—and this alone was the reason for our unfortunate reaction. Isn't it true that a good night's sleep and rest can often put problems right which loom so large in the darkness?

TUESDAY—AUGUST 4.

IN Liff Road, Dundee, is Wellburn, one of the happiest eventide homes I have ever visited.

It stands in a peaceful spot amid tall trees, and I know that every one of the old folk who stay there thinks the world of the nuns who do such a splendid job of looking after them.

Well, it seems someone else must have been hearing about the good work done at Wellburn, for something happened there that, I think, must be unique in the history of eventide homes. One of the Fraserburgh fishing boats landed a sturgeon, which, as you know, is by tradition a royal fish. As always, it was offered to the Queen—and what do you think? By her command, it was sent to Wellburn.

Goodness, it was the first time the nuns had ever seen a sturgeon, let alone set about cooking one. What's more, the thing was nearly six feet long! But, led by the indefatigable Mother Superior, cook it they did—and there was enough to give all the old folk a big helping. Of course, they knew the Queen had sent it to them, and that made it an even bigger thrill, so a letter was sent to Buckingham Palace, to let the Queen know how much they had enjoyed it.

More than once someone in an eventide home has told me that they're treated like royalty. After hearing about the royal sturgeon, I can well believe it!

WEDNESDAY—AUGUST 5.

I WALKED with care a lonely lane
When day was almost done,
The hedges green, the fields serene,
And bright the setting sun.
A late lark sang against the sky,
And carefree as his song was I.

THE FRIENDSHIP BOOK

THURSDAY—AUGUST 6.

WHEN William Boyle appeared in an interview on TV, his wife, Sybil, was naturally very proud. Next morning she could not resist asking when she was at the tailor's —" Did you see my husband last night and how did he look?"

The tailor considered this problem. " Yes," he answered, " I saw it and it was very nice. Mr Boyle's shoulders were sitting fairly well and I don't think I ever saw better lapels . . ."

Isn't it true that we all see things at first wholly from our own point of view?

FRIDAY—AUGUST 7.

WHEN I called recently on the Lamberts packing chests were lying about in the hall. " Doing a moonlight?" I inquired. " Off to West Africa," they told me, " sailing on Thursday week. But we shall be back in twelve months."

Seeing my next unspoken question, Graham answered it for me. " At my present hospital job," he explained, " we certainly have enough to do, but in West Africa I shall be seeing cases as they used to be in this old country, cases which have gone untreated for years. These are things which my students can only read about in a textbook. If I cannot do much to help the worst patients in West Africa, at least it should make me a better surgeon."

You may have guessed by this time that Graham Lambert (or so we shall call him) is a consultant surgeon in a very great hospital. And you might have been excused for thinking that in his line he probably understood all there was to know. Perhaps this new adventure helps to explain his already splendid life of achievement.

SATURDAY—AUGUST 8.

YOU are never so poor that you can't help others.

Kitty Wilkinson learned the simple creed from her mother, and she lived by it. A humble factory worker, she raised her family amid the poverty of the Liverpool slums, where her kindness was a by-word. Many a time she worked wonders with bread and soup unequalled since the miracle of the loaves and fishes!

She remained true to her creed even when the plague of cholera struck Liverpool, for she went wherever she was needed, heedless of the risk she ran of catching the dread disease herself. It was on those errands of mercy she realised how shared bedding helped to spread the killer germ. But how could it be kept clean when her neighbours were too poor to buy fuel to fire a wash-tub?

So, out of her compassion for others, sprang her great idea. She collected half a dozen wash-tubs and put them in a cellar. She got money from a benevolent society to buy fuel and chloride of lime. And before the week was out, women were lining up at the cellar door with their washing. In this way the first " steamie " was born.

If you visit the great Liverpool Cathedral today you will find that among the soaring stained-glass windows is one depicting a woman with a washing basket, and children clinging to her skirts.

It's dedicated to Catherine Wilkinson, truly the angel of the wash-tub.

SUNDAY—AUGUST 9.

WOE unto him that buildeth his house by unrighteousness, and his chambers by wrong; that useth his neighbour's service without wages, and giveth him not for his work.

THE FRIENDSHIP BOOK

MONDAY—AUGUST 10.

MY friend, John G. Bunney, of Consett, sent me this bit of homely philosophy, and I am happy to pass it on to you—

Money will buy a bed but not sleep,
Books but not brains,
Food but not appetite,
Finery but not beauty,
A house but not a home,
Medicine but not health,
Luxuries but not culture,
Amusement but not happiness,
A church pew but not heaven.

Makes you think? And how true it is.

TUESDAY—AUGUST 11.

SOMEHOW, with the uncanny instinct of a child, young Duncan Nixon, of Dumbarton, in a few words of utter simplicity, has summed up all that our faith is really about.

Duncan was asked what, in his opinion, heaven was like. And here is what he said—

Heaven is for good people. Every time you do a good thing to somebody, a brick goes on your house in heaven.

I wonder if by what you and I did today, the walls of our heavenly homes have risen any higher?

WEDNESDAY—AUGUST 12.

SUCH a lot of people
Toiling in the sun—
Waitresses and shop girls
Always on the run.
Such a lot of folk, I say,
Work while you're on holiday!

THURSDAY—AUGUST 13.

YOU know, it really is a good thing to be alone sometimes.

It's exciting to be with a crowd. That's part of the fun of a holiday—being one of a gay company aboard a cruising liner, having a caravan among another hundred caravans, going to the theatre, romping on the seashore, or jostling along at a place you've never visited before—all this is at least part of the essence of a holiday.

But isn't there something to be said for being alone? . . . walking on the pier so early in the morning that you have it all to yourself!

And thinking a bit, taking a look at things, asking yourself if you are the man or woman you really want yourself to be.

There's a lot to be said for being alone with your thoughts—now and then.

FRIDAY—AUGUST 14.

IF you think you are beaten—you are;
  If you think you dare not—you don't;
If you like to win but you think you can't,
  It's almost certain you won't.
If you think you'll lose—you've lost;
  For out of the world we find—
Success begins with a fellow's will,
  It's all in the state of mind.
If you think you're outclassed—you are;
  You've got to think high to rise;
You've got to be sure of yourself
  Before you can win a prize.
Life's battles don't always go
  To the strongest or fastest man;
But soon or late the man who wins
  Is the man who thinks he can.

OUT OF DOORS

There's no air like the country air,
Rich as heather honey;
You cannot buy a scent as sweet
For any kind of money.

DAVID HOPE

SERVICE WITH A SMILE

There's one in every village
All up and down the land,
A little shop, beloved of bairns,
Someone to understand.
Bless them all, through all their days,
For their homely, sympathetic ways.

DAVID HOPE

THE FRIENDSHIP BOOK

ANDREW had no university degrees, for he left school at 15.

But, in his own quiet way, he was a philosopher. He worked hard, learned much, and lived simply, and many a man who had taken a wrong turning found a job with him, for he always believed in giving someone another chance.

I don't think he was ever let down—and part of the reason lay in something he said to all those to whom he gave a second chance.

It was simply this—*Whatever your past has been, always remember you have a spotless future.*

We can all make a fresh start—any time.

LEARN to do well ; seek judgment, relieve the oppressed, judge the fatherless, plead for the widow.

A FRIEND sends me a few lines now and then— always witty and always welcome. Almost always he begins with prose and ends with a neat bit of verse . . . I will not style it poetry, nor would he.

The other day my friend told me he was home again after attending a small conference in which, he declared, he was conspicuous for not making any major speech. And then follows this wee verse :

I'm afraid I am not a good speaker—
    My friends with this fact will agree.
The reason I fail is quite simple :
    My friends won't stop talking to me !

TUESDAY—AUGUST 18.

ONE night Mrs Jack Waldie, of Ceres, travelled to London by bus from Edinburgh. And she passed this story about the journey on to me.

Between nine and ten o'clock, somewhere near the Borders, the relief driver went to the front of the bus. As he did so, the bus slowed down, and both he and the driver leaned forward and waved furiously out into the darkness. Immediately afterwards the bus picked up speed again.

As the relief driver returned, he smiled and said, "Well, that's No. 1 old lady!" And he explained to the puzzled passengers that for years every driver on the Edinburgh-London run has slowed his bus at her lonely cottage and waved to her. Always, she is at her window waiting to wave back. He added that farther down the road was "No. 2"—and, sure enough, a few miles later, the two drivers waved to an old body waiting at her window.

Nobody I've asked knows how it all started, and I don't suppose any of the drivers has ever met the two old ladies. Yet it has become a grand tradition—a kind of tryst, over in a moment, but leaving behind warm hearts and smiles.

WEDNESDAY—AUGUST 19.

WHEN I was small, long, long ago,
*   This month meant much to me—*
Escape from school and streets and chores
*   To freedom by the sea.*
How I would dash to make a splash;
*   With what excited hands*
I built my castle—flag-bedecked—
*   And laughed on tide-washed sands.*
Now, looking back, I think at seven
*   I found the sandy side of heaven!*

THE FRIENDSHIP BOOK

A FRIEND remarked a few days ago, "We're never happy except when looking back." Frankly, I am not at all sure he is right—but at any rate there is an element of truth in it.

So often the anxiety of catching a train or driving along a busy road, keeping an eye on the children, makes your pleasures seem less than perfect at the time.

And then, one wet, windy day, you have a mental flashback, and realise what a happy week you had at Blackpool or in Switzerland.

You enjoy a remembered highlight and forget those tired feet or the rush or anxiety.

It's good to remember happy hours or days—to recall thrills of yesterday or yesteryear.

WATCHING a service on TV some time ago, the Lady of the House and I were delighted to hear the hymn "Count Your Blessings" sung. Some may scoff at it. Some may call it an old-fashioned tub-thumper. But how the folk on TV enjoyed it!

The man who wrote "Count Your Blessings" was Johnson Oatman, a Methodist minister who lived and worked in New Jersey around the turn of the century.

Though he wrote more than 5000 hymns and songs, only one or two are known today. But, in "Count Your Blessings," he struck a chord that still echoes in many thousands of hearts—
When upon life's billows you are tempest tossed,
When you are discouraged, thinking all is lost,
Count your many blessings, name them one by one,
And it will surprise you what the Lord hath done!

THE FRIENDSHIP BOOK

I'D like to tell you about a letter I received from Miss Jane Meldrum, of Laureston Hospital, Castle Douglas.

It wasn't very long. It was written, with difficulty, on cheap, lined notepaper. Yet, when you read it, you'll see why it meant so much to me.

" I want to tell you about my best-ever holiday," Jane wrote. " I have been in hospital for nine years, and on Saturday afternoon one of our good nurses took me out in a chair on to the lawn, and I sat till five o'clock. It was so peaceful—nothing but the birds singing. No holiday could be like it."

Thank God if you've " only " been away for a day here and there. Thank God if you could " only " manage a week this year. And thank God for folk like Jane who, by treasuring their few blessings, humble us into counting our own.

REPENT : for the Kingdom of Heaven is at hand.

THERE must be millions who know the 23rd Psalm, sung to the lovely tune Crimond, especially since the day when it was sung at the wedding of our present Queen. Not so many will know it in the translation of Isaac Watts, which ends with the words put in this way—

There would I find a settled rest,
    While others go and come;
No more a stranger or a guest,
    But like a child at home.

Whatever the version we know, there's something here that touches the heart.

THE FRIENDSHIP BOOK

TUESDAY—AUGUST 25.

A YOUNG man in a neat grey suit made his way with a heavy heart into the crowded kirk at Slamannan, in Stirlingshire.

He had travelled from the South of England to be there, for the service that day was no ordinary one—it was the funeral of the beloved minister of Slamannan, Rev. Sandy Cameron.

For 20 years Mr Cameron had been chaplain at the Polmont Borstal Institution, and I believe he did more to influence the lives of the boys there than anyone ever realised. For he was a man they could respect, a man of forthright honesty who understood the problems that they faced.

He showed the Polmont boys where they'd gone wrong. He reminded them of those whose hearts they had broken. If there was any good in them, and there always was, he found it and treasured it.

The young stranger in the grey suit was once a Polmont boy. There was a time when most folk would have said he was a bad egg. But because of Sandy Cameron, that boy is now in a good job in England, happily married, a fine, honest man.

In many a humble home where a boy once went wrong, the name of Sandy Cameron is nightly blessed. In many a salvaged life, his example is cherished. Of all the tributes he was paid, these, I think, would have meant most to him.

WEDNESDAY—AUGUST 26.

SHE'S old and deaf and nearly blind,
    And yet her face is sweet.
She does not hear, she has to peer,
    When you come from the street.
Life's greatest thrill for her is this—
If lips she loves give her a kiss.

THURSDAY—AUGUST 27.

THE things that children say and do can often be so refreshing.

They keep those of us who are older at least a bit younger in spirit than we should be without them, and sometimes they make us think.

As young Donald did when he wrote this friendly little letter to God—

" Dear God—All of us are going on holiday for a week and I hope it is fine as we need some sun tan; so you won't see us at church, but I hope you will be there when we get back. Do you ever have a holiday? I expect you are too busy.—With love, Donnie."

FRIDAY—AUGUST 28.

ONE Sunday evening a lone figure stood gazing out over the hills of Cheshire.

He was a parson, Rev. John Ellerton, and he was making his way home from the evening service. But, as he turned to look back at his church, his eyes were drawn towards the sky.

It had been a perfect day. Now, as the sun sank in the west, the heavens were ablaze with crimson, gold and purple, breathtaking in its beauty. John stood in silence, thrilled by the splendour of the sunset, then walked slowly on.

All this took place a century ago, but we can still share John's thoughts as he arrived home that night. For he wrote of that sunset, and all it meant to him, in lines that have become one of the most beloved of our evening hymns—

The day Thou gavest, Lord, is ended,
The darkness falls at Thy behest,
To Thee our morning hymns ascended,
Thy praise shall sanctify our rest . . .

THE FRIENDSHIP BOOK

HERE is a comment made by an old farmer to a friend of mine.

The two were watching Sunday evening traffic roaring by the end of a lane. They agreed that most of the cars were travelling too fast—at any rate for their liking. After a pause, the farmer remarked, with a peculiar glint in his eyes, " I must be getting on, laddie. I can remember when I was surprised to see cars driven at only fifteen miles an hour—and I still am !"

THOU art worthy, O Lord, to receive glory and honour and power : for Thou hast created all things, and for Thy pleasure they are and were created.

I'M not saying I believe this, but think about it and make your own conclusion.

Somebody said recently—" The greatest truths are the simplest, and so are the greatest men."

If by " the greatest " we mean the happiest and most useful people, I'm compelled to agree that they are the men or women who require very little to satisfy them, who have a simple creed, who make little of their sorrows or troubles and a great deal of whatever good fortune comes their way, and are brave and cheery when suffering comes.

And, surely, the greatest man who ever lived was simple, though He said the profoundest thing ever said: Love your neighbour as yourself.

SEPTEMBER

TUESDAY—SEPTEMBER 1.

" OH well," I said to myself the other day,
" one man's food is another man's poison."

I suppose, on second thoughts, I ought to have commented—" It's not quite my cup of tea."

For I happened to be reading about tea—neither home brewed nor office nor factory brewed, but tea made in a way I had never dreamed of.

Buddhist monks, it seems, are the world's biggest tea-drinkers, many of them swallowing 70 or more cups of tea a day. It is doubtful, however, if you would care to have tea with any of them. A cup of tea to the monks of Tibet means breaking off a piece of a tea brick—tea leaves, twigs and dust compressed into the shape of a brick, and dropped into a cauldron of cold water. A handful of soda is added, and the water allowed to boil for five or six hours. The mixture is then poured through a strainer into a large urn, and quantities of salt and prime rancid butter added, the brew being well churned. Only after the churning is finished is the brew ready.

I presume the Buddhist monk then pours himself a cup of tea and sips it thoughtfully.

All of which goes to show that it takes all sorts to make a world!

WEDNESDAY—SEPTEMBER 2.

A NOD, a smile, a handshake while
You meet a friend, and talk;
A singing bird, a laugh, a word
With someone as you walk.
What little things of every day,
Yet how they help us on our way!

THURSDAY—SEPTEMBER 3.

GEORGE GIBB told me this story.

It is about an auction sale—of old-fashioned tables and chairs and ornaments and pictures. Among the latter was a framed print of Holman Hunt's famous portrait of Christ as the Light of the World. It shows Him standing, lantern in hand, at the locked door of a house, infinite compassion in His face.

After a few words, the auctioneer suggested one pound, but there was no response. He lowered the price to ten shillings, five shillings, one shilling —still no bidder in the crowd. " Will anybody bid sixpence ?" he urged, and in the stolid silence that followed he put the picture on one side, remarking sadly, " The Man nobody wants."

It is a parable, this old story. How terribly true that nobody wants the Christ who knocks at the door of every heart, yet all this sad, frightened, cruel, bewildered world NEEDS Him, and needs him more now than ever.

FRIDAY—SEPTEMBER 4.

ONE evening last summer an American stopped an elderly man in Leith Walk, Edinburgh, and asked to be directed to an address beyond North Bridge. The Scotsman began trying to direct him, gave it up, and exclaimed, " Och, I'll show ye !"

So the two walked a mile, talking and sharing thoughts. " I'm afraid I've taken you a long way from home," said the stranger.

" Naw, naw," was the reply. " It's nae bother."

Returning to Chicago, the American declared that friendly stroll when a Scotsman went the second mile, was the best thing that happened while he was on holiday.

THE FRIENDSHIP BOOK

WITHOUT knowing it, a shopkeeper preached a sermon by his living and dying.

He worked hard. He bought his small shop on borrowed money, paid back every penny, took over the property next door, reorganised, cut prices, practically lived on the premises seven days a week, did well—and yet did badly.

His wife's health broke down. His children forsook him because he lived for his shop, talked shop, thought shop, did shady things in his business—and crushed his own soul.

Ambition is a fine thing. But there is a great deal more in life—love and home and children and art and music and kindliness and sympathy.

That shopkeeper died before he was fifty. And the sermon he preached was : Don't do as I have done, for I was born a man and died a grocer.

BE thou faithful unto death, and I will give thee a crown of life.

WHEN the time comes, Granpa Parker goes round his garden with a straw basket, picking up all the windfalls from his fruit trees. Many of these are damaged, so he eats them first. The gathered fruit he stores later on in a cool place. But by the time he has finished the windfalls, the first of the later apples and pears are starting to go off, too. The end result is that he eats his quota of doubtful or damaged fruit every day all through the winter !

Perhaps he might be better to enjoy some of the good things of life while they are still fresh !

THE FRIENDSHIP BOOK

TUESDAY—SEPTEMBER 8.

ONE of the most famous of all English essayists was William Hazlitt, who died in 1830. Mostly his days were pleasant—at least his last words are said to have been—"Well, I've had a happy life."

When the time comes, couldn't most of us say the same? There is always much to be thankful for, if only we are willing to search for it.

WEDNESDAY—SEPTEMBER 9.

ARE you lonely and fed up?
*   Just make a cup of tea.*
Nothing like it to dispel
*   Self-pity, you'll agree.*
TWO cups cost but little more.
*   Take them with you—go next door.*

THURSDAY—SEPTEMBER 10.

ON the way home from a meeting one evening I looked up and saw the stars in a clear sky.

At the meeting several speakers had reminded us that the world is in poor shape, that old and honoured beliefs and customs are being swept away and a dangerous malaise has bitten deep into the hearts and souls of millions. It is all something to disturb and challenge.

And there, far above my head, were the silent stars. I called to mind how, during the French Revolution, Jean Bon St Andre, a leader of the rising, laughed in the face of a simple peasant, and boasted: "No more religion now! We'll pull down your steeples so that nothing will be left to remind you of your outworn superstitions."

"Pull them down," replied the peasant calmly. "You cannot help leaving us the stars."

FRIDAY—SEPTEMBER 11.

NOT everybody says grace before meals, but some of those who do may be shocked by a little grace I came upon.

But when you think about it, even the most devout might well recite these lines:—

> Lord, bless the food upon these dishes
> As Thou didst bless the loaves and fishes.
> And like the sugar in our tea
> May all of us be stirred by Thee.

SATURDAY—SEPTEMBER 12.

HER father started the business and Miss Smith has just retired from a shop which, as the only unmarried daughter, she carried on until now. Through more than half a century and two world wars it was the same manufacturer and wholesaler in London who provided much of their supplies. But Miss Smith felt as retiral drew near that things were now so impersonal that this long association would be forgotten, and she would disappear unremarked from the business scene.

When the day came and she handed over the keys to another she was astonished to find that the great concern in London had sent up the managing director himself! A surprise dinner had been arranged and there was a piece of jewellery for Miss Smith, as well as a handsome cheque.

Often one feels that some companies are interested only in making money. So it is a pleasure to find that there is still some heart in business.

SUNDAY—SEPTEMBER 13.

SEEK ye the Lord while he may be found, call ye upon him while he is near.

THE FRIENDSHIP BOOK

I HAVE been thinking about Robert Louis Stevenson, the great Scottish writer, and of how the story of his life is a long search for health. He lived in the days before a cure was known for such a sickness as his, and so in quest of health he was to wander as far away as Samoa in the Pacific, where he was to die. Working in between his bouts of illness he was still able to earn his bread. It was at such a time that he wrote one of his prayers.

"We thank Thee for this place in which we dwell; for the love that unites us; for the health, the work, the food, and the bright skies that make our lives delightful; for our friends in all parts of the earth and our friendly helpers in this foreign isle. Give us courage, gaiety, and a quiet mind . . ."

Stevenson might have bemoaned his ill-health or his exile; instead he counts his blessings.

I WAS talking with young Derek the other day. He has left school and has begun his career in industry. Derek is a good lad; but like anyone else of that age he still has a lot to learn. He was saying that among all the opportunities and temptations of his new surroundings he finds it harder to lead a Christian life than when he was still at school. "It isn't easy!" he insisted.

So I asked him, "What big or complex thing was ever easy? Have we who are older found it simple to conquer war? Or to discover a cure for cancer?" The nature of our difficulties and temptations may change as we grow older, but they are with us in some other form to the end of the road. No one who has triumphed ever asserted on looking back that it was an easy way.

WEDNESDAY—SEPTEMBER 16.

IF you have little folk at home
Be gentle, patient, kind.
They're bothersome, but years fly by—
They'll grow up SOON, you'll find.
A day will come when you are old
And need, perhaps, some care.
If they have learned to think of you,
They'll have some love to spare.
Instead of grief they'll bring you joy;
Invest NOW in your girl or boy !

THURSDAY—SEPTEMBER 17.

IT is nineteen hundred years since a Roman writer first told the story of how Cornelia, wife of Sempronius Gracchus, silenced a somewhat overbearing and proud acquaintance.

She was visited one afternoon—so Seneca tells us—by a woman who showed off her jewels, doing it ostentatiously and hoping, thereby, to make Cornelia ashamed of her lack of ornaments, for she was simply though tastefully dressed.

How that woman went on about her jewels—what they cost and which she liked most and why she had chosen to wear the particular ones which adorned her person, and so on.

The quiet, dignified and very gracious Cornelia contrived to keep her guest until her two small boys arrived home from school. Then she introduced her sons, saying pleasantly but with a vast amount of meaning—" These are *my* jewels."

Whether this silenced the noisy guest or not, I cannot say; but the story has survived nearly twenty centuries, and is a reminder that people, even little, unimportant people, are worth much more than riches.

FRIDAY—SEPTEMBER 18.

MRS MAIN was telling me about her minister the other day, and here, without any comment from me, is a piece of what she had to say.

" The worst," she said, " is the point where he closes the Book and says ' Finally . . .' You know that he isn't finished, but that there's another ten minutes to go ! I always feel that when anyone says ' Finally,' they should come to the end, sit down, and shut up !"

SATURDAY—SEPTEMBER 19.

I HAVE always been an admirer of bees.

A bee stung me when I was a small boy, and rather then resent the pain he caused me, I read a book about bees, and came to have a tremendous interest in them.

The other day a bee came to rest on the back of my hand. I kept still. It preened its wings, turned round, and flew off. It was a busy bee, and had much to do.

And this bee reminded me of something I read in a magazine years ago, something written by a keeper of bees named Bradshaw, and to be found on the label of every jar of honey he sells:

Honeybees have gathered nectar from approximately 4,500,000 clusters of clover and have travelled about 150,000 miles (six times round the world) to deliver this jar of honey to you.

You might like to dwell on this the next time you put a little honey on your bread.

SUNDAY—SEPTEMBER 20.

IN quietness and in confidence shall be your strength.

MONDAY—SEPTEMBER 21.

THREE hundred years ago, the little town of Eilenburg, in Germany, was in desperate straits. It had been ravaged by war. Famine had brought its inhabitants to starvation, and now they were stricken by plague.

The minister, Martin Rinkart, saw his brother clergymen carried off one by one. His congregation died by the score. Yet he carried on steadfastly with his work, visiting the sick, and sometimes conducting as many as 50 funerals in a single day.

If any man had cause to be embittered, or to question his faith, Martin did. Yet when the war ended and the plague disappeared, he wrote a hymn of thanksgiving that has become one of the greatest songs of praise the world had ever heard:—

> Now thank we all our God, with heart and hands and voices,
> Who wondrous things hath done, in whom the world rejoices.

TUESDAY—SEPTEMBER 22.

MRS SMITH of Rutherglen gave me a thought some time ago. She reminded me that if ever we pray we have at least some guide as to how to do it sincerely and purposefully.

Hold your right hand before you, as if you were about to pat your chest. Then, your thumb is towards your heart—pray for those you love.

Your index finger points the way—pray for all who direct or guide you. Your middle finger is above two others—pray for all in authority.

Your third, and weakest finger, reminds you to pray for those in sickness, want, and trouble.

Your little finger, the least and last, suggests that you pray for yourself, if there is time.

LIGHTHOUSE RELIEF

Tonight they'll sit by the fireside,
Far from the beat of wind and tide.
But still perhaps through the friendly glow,
They'll see the beacon flash and go,
And hear the Western surges roar,
Round the rocky base of Skerryvore.

DAVID HOPE

COMPENSATIONS

I love the leaves that brush my feet,
Brown and gold and red,
Although the pleasure's bitter-sweet —
The price of summer sped.

DAVID HOPE

THE FRIENDSHIP BOOK

WEDNESDAY—SEPTEMBER 23.

COULD your next-door neighbour be
*   Ill or weather-bound,*
Lonely, anxious—waiting for
*   You to call round?*
Why not take her unawares—
*   Be the answer to her prayers?*

THURSDAY—SEPTEMBER 24.

ONE day, a year or two ago, an elderly man
approached the door of a church.

When he found a wedding was about to take
place, he turned to leave. But one of the ushers saw
him, and told him he was welcome to stay, and the
minister, Mr Mitchell, went forward to greet him.

Still the stranger hesitated, then, quietly, he
revealed that he had been freed that very morning
from prison. Mr Mitchell told him that made
no difference. He was still welcome. The man's
back straightened. " Then, sir," he said. " I must
make the bride a present."

Of course, he had nothing to give so instead he
asked that the organist might play the tune of his
favourite hymn, " By Cool Siloam." It had been a
comfort to him all his life, even in prison. Now it
would be his gift to the bride on her wedding day.

While the unknown guest found a seat, Mr
Mitchell had a word with the organist. And so, just
before the wedding march, to the surprise of
everyone, the soft strains of the lovely old tune
spread through the kirk.

        Dependent on Thy bounteous breath,
        We seek Thy grace alone . . .
        To keep us still Thine own . . .

What more perfect prayer could there be for a
bride—or for a man just out of prison?

THE FRIENDSHIP BOOK

SHE'S much sweeter now.

I refer to Maisie. I used to admire her several years ago. Who could help it? She was brilliant scholastically. She dressed most successfully——always way ahead of fashion. She had a fine face, chin tilted. And all the money she needed came out of father's pocket. I just wished that Maisie were not quite so snooty, a trifle more sympathetic.

And then that illness, leading to an operation. And afterwards. Things did not go quite right at first, and she needed nursing in a surgical ward; and one night she wanted to turn on her side, *and couldn't.* Maisie, who could do everything, and do it well! In the end she simply had to call for the night nurse, and ask to be made more comfortable. And, oh, how it hurt her to feel inadequate! But it did her a world of good.

I said at first; she's sweeter now!

DURING 1968, some alterations and additions were made to London Airport. And one of the innovations was a chapel.

It may seem odd at first, a chapel in the middle of a busy airport. Yet, when you think of it, is there anywhere it is more needed? Thirteen million people pass through London Airport every year, and there daily one can see the great dramas of life—the sad partings—loved ones reunited —the first step towards a new life in a new land.

I may be wrong, but I believe that chapel is a blessing to many—the anxious who pray for safety, relatives who commit their loved ones into God's keeping . . . and the grateful ones who give thanks at journey's end.

SUNDAY—SEPTEMBER 27.

MAN doth not live by bread only, but by every word that proceedeth out of the mouth of the Lord doth man live.

MONDAY—SEPTEMBER 28.

LAWRENCE MACKAY was the butcher's boy in the village of Balfron. He lived with his mother and father and two young brothers, a tall, fair-haired, laughing lump of a lad without an enemy in the world.

He was one of those folk who simply couldn't help seeing the cheery side of things. No matter how down in the dumps a customer might be, the merry smile of the butcher's boy soon chased the blues away. The old folk especially loved to hear his knock at the door, for he always had time for a chat and a joke with them.

Then, tragically, Lawrence was killed in a road accident. It seemed unbelievable that his smile would never be seen again, and that his friendly figure would no longer come whistling up the garden path. In the shop next morning, housewives stood with tears running down their faces when the news was broken to them.

Lawrence was laid to rest in the cemetery on the hilltop. The church was so crowded that many who wanted to join in the service had to stand outside the door, and at the last, the whole village seemed to be around his grave . . . titled folk from the big houses, farmers, mothers, and grannies, all wondering why it had to be.

That is a question no one can answer—but, in a way, the life of this butcher's boy was a challenge to us all, and the best tribute anyone can pay him is to meet that challenge as cheerfully as he did.

TUESDAY—SEPTEMBER 29.

IN one Scottish church, the minister, Mr Sandy McDonald, usually takes something into the pulpit to illustrate his children's talk.

Sometimes it's a toy. Sometimes it's a household article. Always he uses it in a wonderful way to give point to what he says. But one week, he told the children he had nothing to show them, so he'd just come down beside them and have a chat with them.

His story was fascinating. It captured their attention at once, and held it all the way through. Then, after the children's hymn, Mr McDonald returned to the pulpit and watched the little ones move off to the Sunday school in the hall.

Suddenly, one wee lad turned round and, with a friendly grin, shouted to the minister in the most pally of voices, "Cheerio!" It was the minister's turn to smile. "Cheerio," he called back—and in a moment everyone in the church was smiling, too, warmed by the glow of the friendly exchange.

Isn't it wonderful how, in all innocence, a child can so often spread brightness and joy in the simplest of ways?

WEDNESDAY—SEPTEMBER 30.

IT'S what you do, not what you say,
Your watchful children spot.
No sermons, please; your kids can see
How very good you're NOT.
It's your example shapes young lives,
It's how you act each day . . .
It's useless saying, "Don't do that,"
If that's the game YOU play.
I must repeat: It's what you do
That makes them love what's good and true.

OCTOBER

ONE elderly lady I know had little money to spare, but she saved up and treated herself to a budgie. That little blue gentleman has cheered and entertained her for two years now and he is still chattering away nineteen to the dozen.

Another lonely old soul sits or stands at her windows and waves or smiles to everyone going by—and now and then someone looks in for a chat.

A third lonely person, blessed with moderate health, pops in to see her neighbours.

She has the wit to stay no more then a few minutes, which means that she is never a bother . . . but she always gathers sufficient gossip and news to keep her thinking a while.

There are more lonely folk than you might think—and loneliness is never pleasant. But even though you are old and live alone, there are ways of not being lonely.

I WAS pondering a letter about a baby saved by the kiss of life when a thought came to me.

I reached down my Bible, turned the pages, came to the Second Book of Kings, chapter four, and I read—

" And when Elisha was come into the house, the child was dead, and laid upon his bed. Elisha went in, therefore, shut the door, and prayed. And he put his mouth on the child's mouth, and his eyes upon his eyes, and his hands upon his hands . . . and the child sneezed seven times, and opened his eyes."

Is there indeed anything new under the sun ?

THE FRIENDSHIP BOOK

IT'S so easy to take people for granted, especially if they've become so much part of the scene you hardly notice them.

I'm thinking of Mrs Elsie Macpherson, of Kingussie. For as long as anyone could recall, she'd been cleaner at the town hall and council offices. And because she arrived after everyone had gone home, few ever saw her cleaning, scrubbing the stairs, and polishing the floors.

And few can have realised just how long she had worked there—a whole fifty years.

She began as a young woman, because her husband was blind and money was short. And though, as the years passed, she became a widow, and her family left home, she kept on faithfully. Then, one night, at the age of 78 she wrung out her washing cloth, put away her pail, and, with a proud look at the spotless offices, closed the door behind her.

It was the last time she ever did so, for a day or two later she fell seriously ill. Even then, she didn't forget her duties. One of the last things she did was to send her daughter to the office in her place, and one of the last things she said was, " Mind and put out the bins for the dustmen." Soon after, she passed away.

So, today, I honour the faithful cleaner of Kingussie, whose greatest pride was to do her lifetime's task well, and whose humble example challenges us all.

CHARITY suffereth long, and is kind ; charity envieth not ; charity vaunteth not itself, is not puffed up.

THE FRIENDSHIP BOOK

MONDAY—OCTOBER 5.

I HAVE been pondering a survey which someone made of a thousand famous and successful men to discover how they got their start in life.

It is, I think, interesting to note that—in round figures—300 began on farms, etc., 200 by selling newspapers, and 200 as messenger boys. 100 were apprentices, 100 went first into factories and 50 began on the railways.

That adds up to 950. What about the other 50? They, and only they, had well-to-do parents to give them a start.

It seems that, as a rule, you have to work hard and long to get anywhere and be somebody.

TUESDAY—OCTOBER 6.

MOTHER was almost at the end of a big wash. She had a basket of wet clothes which had been on the line once, and brought in because of rain. She was going out to the green with it again when her wee girl, in the next room, called, " Mummy, will you come and look at the house I've drawed ?"

Try as she would, the tired housewife could not refrain from putting an edge on her reply. " Oh, all right," she called back irritably. " I'll come in a minute."

Instantly a childish voice asked, " Do you mean one of your minutes or one of mine ?"

Yes, often Mum's so busy she feels she can't break off and look at a child's drawing or listen to a child's story or show interest in a child's doings. Yet, come to think of it, no chore in the house is quite as important as helping her bairn to grow up happily and in the right way.

It's in the odd minutes that mother and child build up a pattern of life.

WEDNESDAY—OCTOBER 7.

Y OU don't need wealth or high renown
To make a body smile,
To warm her heart and banish aches
And loneliness awhile.
Just lift the latch and, smiling, say—
" Now, Granny, how are you today ?"

THURSDAY—OCTOBER 8.

JOHNNY DONNELLY'S home is in the village of Wilkieston, Midlothian, where his wife is postmistress.

If you step into the Post Office the chances are you'll find Johnny behind the counter. He's a cheerful man who'll serve you in a twinkling with whatever you ask for, whether it's a newspaper, tin of beans, pound of ham, or a fourpenny stamp. After that he'll take your money and pass over your change without a moment's hesitation.

Now, so far it may seem there's nothing out of the ordinary about all this. But let me add that Johnny lost his sight in 1946 at the age of 23 while serving with the Army in Germany. Ever since, he's been blind.

You'd never guess it to look at him. You can't tell by the way he moves about the shop or slices the ham or handles the money. Indeed, more than once a stranger has been served by Johnny and gone away without realising he can't see.

Of course, Johnny would give much to have his sight again and to be able to see his wife and children for the first time. But he decided long ago not to dwell on what might have been and instead to meet the challenge with a spring in his step.

Five minutes in his company will tell you how magnificently he has succeeded.

FRIDAY—OCTOBER 9.

IT happened, so I'm told, in one of our big city stations.

A little boy of 11 came skidding round the ticket barrier, and dashed headlong down the platform to catch his train home from school. Alas, he missed it by seconds.

As he stood ruefully watching the train disappear, a porter said sympathetically, " If you'd run faster, son, you'd have made it."

The boy snorted, " I ran fast enough," said he. " I just didn't start soon enough !"

After you've smiled, think about it !

SATURDAY—OCTOBER 10.

ON an island in a certain lovely lake I know, stands a perfect circle of tall pine trees. Heather grows here, too, and a mass of white heather. Looking closely one can see the rather more rare sundew. This little island is a small botanic garden in itself. But I wonder who it was that planted the circle of pines so carefully ?

The answer must be that someone, perhaps a hundred years ago, paused and thought of the future. After a recent gale I noticed that while a certain estate in another place had been compelled to clear away much of the timber, they had deliberately left the best of the tall trees which still lined both sides of the road. Again, someone was thinking ahead.

Just so there are some who think of the children and all who will come after them, while others do not. We can look at our fine churches, splendid libraries, and stout bridges, reflecting that they did not say, " We'll just build for our own time and the future can look after itself." They built for the future, too. And we, in our day, should do no less.

THE FRIENDSHIP BOOK

AND the work of righteousness shall be peace ; and the effect of righteousness quietness and assurance for ever.

JOHN WILSON, known to his friends as the Bard o' Bogmonie, has a verse to remind us that life is not always easy for others. He puts it into four challenging lines—

That wifie, toiling up the stair,
May give you but a passing stare.
Be slow to think she is unkind—
She's loads of trouble on her mind.

HAVE you heard this story about Sir Harry Lauder? One night, when he was on tour, a Salvation Army girl came into the hotel where he and his wife were staying, a sheaf of " War Cry " newspapers in her arms.

Sir Harry approached her. " Lassie," he said with a smile, " if I put a shilling in your tin, will ye lend me your bonnet for twa or three minutes ? "

The girl was mystified. But she untied it, and watched him take it away upstairs.

Within a few minutes he was back, and as he returned it to her he explained that, as a young man of 20, he'd wooed and won a Salvation Army lassie. She'd never looked bonnier than in her Army bonnet —and now, years later, he had asked her to wear it once again, so he might see her as she was when they first met.

Need I add that the offering Sir Harry slipped into the tin was much more than a shilling ?

WEDNESDAY—OCTOBER 14.

SUPPOSE you're sorry for yourself
(Maybe you've an excuse)
Don't dwell too long on all your ills,
Don't think that you're no use.
Find somebody worse off than you—
There must be something you can do!

THURSDAY—OCTOBER 15.

ONE Saturday the Lady of the House was pottering in the garden when three terrors popped up behind the wall, each pointing a clothes-peg at her as they announced, " We're baddies ! Hands up!"

My wife, showing great presence of mind in this surprise hold-up by young Jimmie, Janet and Jean, who sometimes visit their granny next door, put up her hands.

" We're gonna shoot you," the baddies declared.

" Right-oh !" said the Lady of the House. " Will you have a sweetie first ?"

The baddies chorused, " Yes," and climbed over the wall. Indoors they trooped, helped themselves to sweets in the tin box in the living-room, asked who the man in the next room was, and were having a royal time when their granny called over the wall it was time for home. " Oh," exclaimed wee Jean, " we've forgotten to shoot her !"

" Never mind," replied her brother, " let her live till morning !"

FRIDAY—OCTOBER 16.

I FOUND this thought in a magazine. I pass it on to you without comment.

Growing old does not seem so bad when you consider the alternative.

SATURDAY—OCTOBER 17.

ONE Sunday morning a lonely old man was walking through Clydebank, his faithful collie dog trotting by his side.

It was a minute or two before eleven o'clock, and in the distance the man heard the bells of Faifley Church. He hadn't set foot in a kirk for more than 20 years, yet he was drawn by the sound of the bells —and found himself longing to go to church again.

By the time he reached the door, the service had started. Besides, he had his dog with him. Yet, as he listened to the congregation singing the opening hymn, he felt more than ever that he wanted to join them. So, with his dog at his heels, he opened the door, took off his bonnet, and slipped into the back pew.

It was only when the minister, the Rev. James Mitchell, was leaving at the end of the service, that he noticed the old man and his dog. He stopped and spoke. The stranger told him how he'd come to be there—and said he'd like to come back. The minister smiled. " Come whenever you like," he said. " And bring your dog with you !"

As the old man thanked the minister, his eyes glistened. The warmth of the welcome had touched him—and, sure enough, every Sunday since then he has been in his place, his collie dog curled up quietly beneath the pew.

Oh, I know some will say a kirk's no place for a dog, and maybe they're right. But I'm glad there are folk like the minister of Faifley who can see into an old man's heart.

SUNDAY—OCTOBER 18.

I AM Alpha and Omega, the beginning and the end, the first and the last.

MONDAY—OCTOBER 19.

STANDING at the farmhouse door, we looked out across the fields. Tom Borthwick has now taken over another 280 acres of arable land to add to his already considerable dairy farm. " But it wasn't always like this, Francis," Tom assured me. Indeed, I already knew that his father had been but a poor working man, and how as a laddie young Tom had determined to be a farmer.

" I started my herd," he told me, " buying them one at a time at the marts and buying nothing but *kickers*." " What is a *kicker*?" I inquired. " You could buy them for next to nothing," he answered. " They were cows which were good enough, but difficult to milk. I milked them all myself, night and morning."

How often the way to success lies in turning difficulties into opportunities !

TUESDAY—OCTOBER 20.

I KNOW a gallant old soul—a Mrs Martindale— who lives alone although she is 81 and very stiff and, as she says, " creaky." Two world wars took their toll of her nearest and dearest. Her husband died long ago. Three sons are buried overseas.

Her daughter in Australia is married, and has invited her mother to live with them down under.

But the proud, independent body still keeps on in her own small house, living on her pension.

" I'm lucky," she always says. " I have one good neighbour. As long as she pops in, lends a hand with the shopping, tells me the news, and has a cup of tea now and again with me . . . well, I can manage. I have a lot to be thankful for !"

Some folk have a lot and don't know it. Others have very, very little, but make the most of it.

THE FRIENDSHIP BOOK

> *I HAD a little, sleepy bulb.*
> *I hid it in a pot.*
> *It grew until its scented blooms*
> *Cheered my sad heart a lot.*
> *But when I gave my plant away*
> *An old, lone body smiled all day.*

AT first, when Mrs Margaret Burke began to suffer from backache, she simply shrugged it off and carried on with her housework. But, unhappily, it was no ordinary backache, for soon Mrs Burke's legs were paralysed. Ever since, she has been unable to walk a single step.

All that happened years ago, but from the very start Mrs Burke was determined that, even if she'd to live the rest of her life in a wheelchair, she would do her best to be a real mother to her three young children. And how magnificently she has succeeded.

She has taught herself to do all her housework from her wheelchair. She cooks the meals, sets the table, washes up, and dusts the house. She sweeps the floors, scrubs out the kitchen with a pail of water balanced on the footrest of her chair, and makes the beds with the help of a broomstick.

If you were to visit her house any evening, you'd find it just like any other happy home—the bairns sitting in front of the fire in their pyjamas, and Mum tidying up and finishing off all the odds and ends in the kitchen.

Any mother of three will tell you that, at times, life can be a handful. You can imagine how much more so it is for Mrs Burke. Yet, bless her, she has made up her mind she'll jolly well make the best of things as they are.

FRIDAY—OCTOBER 23.

SOME good things come from the other side of the Atlantic—and one of them is this thought passed on by Mrs Atherton, of Windsor, Ontario.

It prompts a smile. But at the same time, it's usually the plain and honest truth :—

If you could kick the person responsible for most of your troubles, you wouldn't be able to sit down for six months !

SATURDAY—OCTOBER 24.

THE girl was lying there, unconscious, on the road just beyond a bend. Her bicycle lay beside her and another girl was bending over the still figure. As we were almost the first on the scene, I hauled the car off on to the grass at the roadside. Meantime, the Lady of the House hurried across with the first-aid kit which we keep in the car. Fortunately, the girl came back to consciousness in a few minutes and she appeared to be uninjured.

What seemed at first sight to be a serious accident had resulted from no more than the entanglement of two bicycles. Going on our way about half an hour later, I could not but reflect how quickly every passing car and lorry had stopped, how willing everyone was to help, and how relieved we all were to find that it was not too serious. They can say what they like, there is still much fundamental good—far more good than bad—in the heart of humanity.

SUNDAY—OCTOBER 25.

KNOW ye that the Lord He is God : it is He that hath made us, and not we ourselves ; we are His people, and the sheep of His pasture.

THE FRIENDSHIP BOOK

MONDAY—OCTOBER 26.

IT'S neat. It's concise. It's true.

So true, in fact, that it's worth keeping in mind every day as we go along life's road.

It needs careful reading, watching the commas:—
We are not what we think we are, but what we think, we are.

TUESDAY—OCTOBER 27.

THE famous surgeon was on a lecture tour of university medical faculties and the pace was beginning to tell.

" I'd give anything for a night off," he told his driver.

" Why don't we swap places, then," the driver suggested. " I've heard you deliver the lecture so often that I could do it myself."

Gratefully the surgeon accepted. Relaxing at the back of the hall at their next stop, he watched the driver make a magnificent job of the lecture. But at question time, to the surgeon's horror, a keen, young doctor raised an extremely difficult point. However, the stand-in never faltered.

" I'm surprised that such a simple point should give you trouble," he told the student.

" It's so simple, in fact, that I'll get my driver, sitting in the back of the hall there, to answer it !"

WEDNESDAY—OCTOBER 28.

IT doesn't sound at all profound,
And yet it's very true
That, come what may each cruel day,
A song will see you through.
For when a gallant pilgrim sings
His happy feet are shod with wings.

THE FRIENDSHIP BOOK

IN the dim lighting of a Chinese restaurant a lady and her husband enjoyed an unusual meal. Near the door, by the cash desk, sat an elderly Oriental with a long and straggling grey beard. When the couple came to pay their bill, the lady said, " This is a nice restaurant and I think everything about it is charming. I think you are charming, too !" The old man smiled before he answered, " I ought to be. I'm nearly eighty years old !" Is it not perfectly true what this old man said ; that as we grow older we should become more and more worth knowing ?

FRIDAY—OCTOBER 30.

I LIKE this story told by the Queen about the time she knighted round-the-world yachtsman Alec Rose.

" He's the only new knight who has instantly obeyed me," the Queen says. " I dubbed him and said—' Rise, Sir Alec '—and Sir Alec Rose !"

SATURDAY—OCTOBER 31.

THIS story came from Miss Olive Upward, of Girton.

A boy of five was taken to an Anglican church service for the first time. He joined in loudly with " Our Father "— not realising that, by tradition, the Lord's prayer would end at " deliver us from evil."

When it dawned on him that everyone else had finished the prayer, and he was the only one carrying on, he turned to his mother and cried, " What have they done with the power and the glory, Mum ?"

Yes, son, it's a question a lot of people are asking these days !

NOVEMBER

SUNDAY—NOVEMBER 1.

WHEN He, the Spirit of Truth, is come, He will guide you into all truth.

MONDAY—NOVEMBER 2.

WILLIAM WOULDHAVE lived in South Shields, but he wasn't a sailor.

He taught singing and worked as a house-painter to make a living. But one thing appalled him—the number of lives lost off the stormy east coast.

Often, deep in thought, he stood at the water's edge, gazing out to the horizon. Any boat that went out to answer a call for help in angry seas must be doubly safe, he told himself—so safe it wouldn't capsize even in the worst storm. Then home he went and tried to devise such a boat.

He fashioned model after model, but, alas, none would work. Then one day, after yet another disappointment, he walked out of the house, wondering if it was all worth while. Soon he came on a woman he knew, drawing water from a well. He sat down on the edge of the well, and as he chatted he idly turned over a broken wooden cup that floated in the woman's pail. Suddenly he realised that, because of its shape, the cup wouldn't float upside down, but immediately righted itself.

At that moment he knew his struggle was over. A few months later the model of the first self-righting lifeboat was in his hands.

It is on his chance discovery that lifeboats are still based. And though William, poor as he was, refused to take a penny for his invention, he knew thousands of lives would be saved because of it.

I am proud to salute him.

THE FRIENDSHIP BOOK

ONE evening recently I walked a mile or two under myriads of stars.

And I found myself asking—" Where have all the stars come from ? When did they come into being ? What keeps them in their vast courses ?

I recalled, years ago, reading about a lecture given by Frank Jeffries, astronomer and scientist. " Friends," he said, addressing his spellbound audience, " the greatest thinkers throughout the ages, including modern times, have utterly failed to give a satisfactory explanation as to how and when this world came into existence. Whatever theory they have worked on, they have eventually come face to face with the necessity of a First Cause which they cannot define; so for ever they stumble along—and all the time, walking patiently behind them, hoping they will turn and look Him in the face, *is* the First Cause, the Lord God of heaven and earth !"

So there, alone with the stars and their Maker, I realised afresh that however unfashionable it may be the Book of Genesis gets amazingly near the truth— *In the beginning, God.*

> *OF ills I've got an awful lot.*
> *I've worries by the score.*
> *I'm just about fed up, flat out—*
> *Life tries me more and more.*
> *But when I think what ills I'm spared,*
> *I shake myself and say:*
> *" There's heaps I should be thankful for*
> *Today and every day.*
> *I'm not in jail ! I have no cough !*
> *Good Lord, I might be MUCH worse off !"*

THE FRIENDSHIP BOOK

IN the centre of the cinema, not too far from the front, there always sits a group of pensioners. Among the first to arrive, they are in their places before the lights dim for the start of the evening programme. However much the price of the other seats may have risen, the charge for a pensioner is still no more than a shilling. After seeing one of my favourite films the other night I came away with the proprietor and his wife as they locked up. But old Bill came with us, too, and got into the owner's car. Bill lives in an Eventide Home and once a week he comes out for this special treat ; never forgetting to say when they drop him at the gate—often after 11 p.m.—" Thanks for a marvellous night out !"

Once they made the mistake of offering him his seat free of charge ; but then they found that he was fiercely independent. It's a thing one notices about the older generation. They are not too keen on free hand-outs, having been reared and trained in the days when you had to work for anything you received.

IN church one Sunday I heard the minister preach about what he positively believed. It was perfectly clear, straightforward, and simple. If more would do this same thing, our hesitant age might go flocking back to church—and this one wasn't exactly empty. Far too many seem to prefer raising doubts, hesitancies and difficulties. Far too many talk about the differences that divide them from other denominations in the same faith. If they would speak instead about where they were agreed, which in all conscience is wide enough, the world might be a happier place.

THE FRIENDSHIP BOOK

IF you think folk couldn't care less about others these days, read this !

One day an Edinburgh pensioner, Mrs Mary Henretty, set off on holiday with her husband. Mrs Henretty can only get about very slowly—and with the aid of a stick at that. So she left home in plenty of time to catch the train from Waverley Station.

At least, she *thought* she had plenty of time, but when she did reach Waverley it was almost train time. She couldn't hurry, of course, so it looked as if she'd miss the train after all.

But her plight hadn't gone unnoticed—far from it. From nowhere, it seemed, four smiling porters appeared with a rattling, railway luggage barrow. " Don't worry," they told her, " we'll get you to the train all right." Gently they helped her on to the barrow, then, with a quick look to see she was secure and comfortable, they set off at a gallop, one at each corner of the barrow, heading for the platform where her train was ready to leave.

As they clattered round the last corner, the guard was about to wave his flag. But he spotted the cavalcade in time, and helped the gallant four to lift Mrs Henretty on to the train. Seconds later it pulled out of the station.

Now I know a luggage barrow is no fairy coach, and I dare say even the lads at Waverley would agree that four white horses would have been more elegant than four cheery porters. But, despite that, Mrs Henretty felt they treated her like a queen.

THE eternal God is thy refuge, and underneath are the everlasting arms.

MONDAY—NOVEMBER 9.

YOU might call this a sermon in five words:—
Faults: husband: quarrel: wife: faults.

And its meaning is this—in a quarrel between a husband and wife, remember there are faults on both sides.

Neat, and true!

TUESDAY—NOVEMBER 10.

AS Remembrance Day draws near once again, this story holds a message for every one of us.

One July day, Mr and Mrs Begg, of Kippen, set off for a tour of the Borders. The weather was perfect, and in the village of Leitholm, in Berwickshire, they stopped to admire a little garden in front of a cottage. It was unlike any garden they had seen before, for the whole of it was ablaze with bright red poppies.

It was a wonderful sight, and they complimented the old lady who lives there on the brave show her poppies made.

She smiled. " It's my way of remembering," she said. Then she went on to explain that, during the 1914-18 War, her sweetheart marched off to fight for his country. He fell in Flanders, and lies in a cemetery there.

But she didn't forget him. She never married, but became a teacher, and devoted her life to the children of the men who *did* come back. Twice she made the pilgrimage to her sweetheart's grave. There she collected poppy seeds, which she planted in her own front garden.

Now, as I say, the Flanders poppies have spread over the whole garden, and as they bloom and fade, they speak of loyalty and faith that have lasted for more than 50 years.

THE FRIENDSHIP BOOK

MY goodness, what a task I'd have
Had I to make a list
Of all the good things in my life,
And not one could be missed!
So long a list of happy things
Should give my soul a whirl of wings!

YOUNG Jimmy McCabe would be the first to admit he'd made a mess of his life.

Perhaps the fault wasn't entirely his. He was put in a home while he was still a baby, and moved to others before he was eight.

Eventually he went to live with a kindly couple at Cuminestown, Aberdeenshire, and it was there he went to school. Oh, he was a handful, and when, at 15, he left to join the Navy, there were those who wondered what would become of him.

He agrees their fears were justified. He was discharged from the Navy. Then, jobless and penniless, he went to Aberdeen. There, in a down-and-outs' breakfast kitchen, he heard someone speak of faith and its power.

That night, as he huddled in a cold street trying to sleep, the words came back to him anew. He sought out a Salvation Army man and poured out the story of his life. Then they knelt in prayer.

That was the turning point in Jimmy's life. Today, in his twenties, he is a different person. He has a steady job. He has found a new purpose in life. He hopes one day to become a minister. And, believe it or not, Jimmy made a return visit to Cuminestown, the place he left under a cloud, to tell the young folk of the power that changed his life. It's a message that will encourage them all.

FRIDAY—NOVEMBER 13.

NOVEMBER it is, and the first sharp frost of the winter. Driving slowly through town, I came upon a line of cars moving slowly behind a lorry which was sanding the road in front to make it safe for the cars which were following. I tagged on to the queue.

Bustling up behind came a big Ford, whose driver, because of a slight bend in the road, could not see what was going on in front. Nothing would do but that he should pull out to pass the lot of us, going fast round the icy corner on the wrong side of the road. It was only by the grace of God that nothing was coming the other way. There could have been a serious accident. What a true saying it is—" Fools rush in where angels fear to tread !"

SATURDAY—NOVEMBER 14.

JUST after breakfast yesterday the Lady of the House said demurely, " Oh, just before you go, Francis, will you move the wardrobe in the bedroom? Only a couple of feet from the wall."

I said I would be glad to. I also asked, " Why ?"

" Just so that I can dust behind it."

" But you can't see the dust if I don't move the wardrobe," I pointed out.

" You're right," she conceded. " *But I know it's there !*"

So I pulled the wardrobe two feet from the wall —and took a bunch of flowers home with me later in the day.

SUNDAY—NOVEMBER 15.

THE Lord is my rock, and my fortress, and my deliverer.

THE KING

Who owns the land, the hills, the tree,
Is all set down in a deed to see.
It's an empty claim, when beneath the pine,
The big stag trumpets " The glen is mine".

DAVID HOPE

PARTNERS

There's dogs for work
And dogs for play,
And some will shirk
And some obey.

But up here, brother,
The creed runs plain,
We trust each other,
And trust again.

DAVID HOPE

AFTER THE FROST

The Ice King passed this way last night
And a dull little pond touched in his flight;
And see, in the morning, for young and for old,
A carpet of magic he's left unrolled.

DAVID HOPE

MONDAY—NOVEMBER 16.

MISS YOUNGSON'S was a sad pilgrimage to see her brother's grave at Anzio, in Italy. Nobody understood a word of her English when she asked them to put her off the bus at the military graveyard. They put her off at a graveyard, but it was the wrong one. The man in charge was able to tell her that she had passed the proper place several miles back. What was she to do? He stopped an enormous lorry and Miss Youngson climbed into its huge cab. But the driver could only take her halfway back. In the end, having stopped at his real destination and consulted with his boss, he took her right to the place she sought. But he would not accept any form of payment.

Perhaps in bygone years he had known some of the gallant men who fought for truth and freedom. Perhaps he was only trying to help a frail little lady. Who can tell? Kind deeds need no explanation.

TUESDAY—NOVEMBER 17.

MRS JEAN CAMPBELL had watched her husband die, had attended the funeral, and now, who but she could go through his wardrobe?

With quiet courage and determination, she carried out the task when alone in the house. And while going through the pockets of a suit, she found a little slip of paper on which her husband had jotted down a reminder—*Order daffodils for Jean.*

Those words compelled her to bite her lip and brush the tears from her eyes. How much she had been loved! How constantly he had thought of her!

" I knew there and then," she told my wife, " that I must not be sorry I had lost him but proud and thankful for all the happy years we had enjoyed together."

THE FRIENDSHIP BOOK

WHEN cold my toes and blue my nose,
And north winds blow my breath away,
I trudge the street on perished feet,
And to myself I say—
" Smile, laddie, smile; and bear in mind
If winter comes, spring's close behind !"

IT is several years since Mr Barr, the minister of Kingussie, retired, but he is still remembered with affection and respect.

He had gone to Kingussie many years before with his wife and three schoolboy sons, John, George and Robin. In his heart he must have dreamed that one of the boys might become a minister, too. But wisely he allowed them all to choose for themselves.

John became an engineer in the development of jet engines, George became an architect, and Robin took a B.Sc. degree in engineering.

If Mr Barr was even a shade disappointed that none of his sons had chosen the ministry, he did not say so. For he was proud of the three boys who had done so well.

But something happened to make him prouder still. His eldest son, John, gave up his secure, comfortable post and went back to university to study for the ministry. Soon after, Robin left his work to do the same. And finally George, too, turned his back on the life he'd made for himself and followed in his father's footsteps.

Now all three are ministers. Their father, now in his eighties, lives in Troon — and who can doubt that his crowning joy is to see his three sons serving the faith to which he devoted his life.

THE FRIENDSHIP BOOK

I TALKED the other day with a philosophical dustman. He is something of a humorist, but now and again he cuts close to the bone.

" Sometimes I don't know what to make of things, Mr Gay," quoth he.

" Take our churches. All of them do good. But after a lot of sermons, they haven't got the world put to rights yet, have they ? Take the law. It untangles some muddles, but it doesn't get very far in making life better, does it ? And the politicians ! We might be better off without them altogether . . .

" Now, consider the dustman, like me. He keeps his corner of the world neat and clean and healthy. But for us, what would this place be like, Mr Gay ?

" We're the boys who tidy up the mess made by other folk and give them some idea of what a pleasant world this could be . . ."

" I wish I hadn't given my hat to a dustman," said I. " I'd have raised it to you right now !"

SOME of us are afraid of being happy.

When you come to think of it, it is really very stupid. We need to carry around with us as much sunshine as we can—it helps to cheer other folk.

I am thinking in this way because of a story related by Mr George Young, sen., of Paisley. He has never forgotten the day, many years ago, when an elderly lady asked how he was.

" Oh," George replied, " I'm not too bad."

" Then why don't you say you're very well ?" snapped the old lady.

Why not, indeed ? If you are ill, say so. If you feel a bit off colour, admit it. But if you are fit as a fiddle, is there any excuse for just being " not too bad ?"

THE FRIENDSHIP BOOK

THE heavens declare the glory of God ; and the firmament sheweth His handywork.

THIS is the time of year when trees are bare, their summer foliage stripped by shrewd winds under dark skies. No one can pretend that life is easy on cold or stormy days and in long and often wild nights. And, whether in summer or winter, all of us have our fears and doubts, our sense of despair and disappointment—all hard things to endure at the best of times.

There comes to mind a challenging proverb from China which says to you and me—*Keep a green branch in your heart, and the singing bird will come.*

It is hard doing it, but worthwhile.

ANDREW CARNEGIE, who was born of poor parents in Dunfermline, died worth no more than five million pounds. Yet he was worth over one hundred millions when he retired eighteen years before his death.

There is no need to tell here his meteoric rise to wealth. He worked in a cotton factory as a boy. He built up the gigantic U.S. Steel Corporation in the course of a tremendously busy and successful career; and then he devoted all his energies to one end—not to making money, but to the hard task of giving it away wisely.

There can be little satisfaction in being the richest man in the cemetery. Making a pile is exciting. Doing something worthwhile with it is abundantly satisfying.

WEDNESDAY—NOVEMBER 25.

WHEN no bird sings in bush or tree,
 And chill the strong winds blow,
There's no point in looking glum
 Or whining if there's snow.
It's when outside the cold mists cling
 That we indoors should sing and sing.

THURSDAY—NOVEMBER 26.

WITH only a month to go before Christmas, I am prompted to pass this story on to you. It came to me from Rev. Victor MacEchern, of Edinburgh, who told me how one Christmas he bought a sprig of mistletoe.

Unable to resist a tease, he asked the young salesgirl, " I know it's seasonal, but what am I supposed to do with mistletoe ?"

The girl glanced archly at Mr MacEchern's clerical collar, then leaned over and whispered, " Take it with you to the Bible Class on Sunday."

I wish he'd told me if he did !

FRIDAY—NOVEMBER 27.

PEOPLE come from all over the world to see the Niagara Falls, and they take away a memory they never forget. But a friend of mine came back from a visit to Niagara with another memory which, to him, was just as unforgettable.

He had a meal there in the Oban Inn restaurant, which, I believe, is run by a Scotsman. On every paper napkin, it seems, there is a thought—just a few words worth pondering. When my friend looked at his napkin, this is what he read:—

" *The easiest person in the world to deceive is yourself.*"

THE FRIENDSHIP BOOK

WE stayed one night recently at a little farm nestling among the trees at the foot of a hillside. All that led us to the place was a rough-painted sign: *Bed & Breakfast*. How we enjoyed the home-made bread, farm milk, butter and cream, and their own cheese!

It was a spot known to many bearded and stoutly-clad climbers coming down from the hills. And looking through the Visitors' Book we found we recognised the names of some of the climbers.

As we sat talking before going to bed, the farmer's wife talked to us about this small enterprise. She told us that she did this work not only for what she can make, but almost as much for the company of her often exciting guests. We work because we have to live. But how much more pleasant that work is if we are bringing pleasure to other folk!

BE strong and of a good courage; be not afraid neither be thou dismayed: for the Lord thy God is with thee, whithersoever thou goest.

HERE'S a thought which some people might do well to contemplate. It comes from the Rev. John Birkbeck, of Aberdeen. Although I first heard it some time ago, it still makes me smile and think hard. Here it is:—

Sitting in a church doesn't turn you into a Christian, any more than sitting in a hen-house turns you into a hen!

DECEMBER

TUESDAY—DECEMBER 1.

HAVE you heard the story of Pietro Bandinelli?
It began more than 450 years ago, when Leonardo da Vinci, the artist, stopped him as he left Milan Cathedral, where he sang in the choir. The artist planned a great picture of the Last Supper. For months, he'd searched for a model for the central figure of Jesus. Now, in the face of young Pietro, he saw the strength, nobility and compassion he'd sought for so long.

So Pietro's face became the face of Jesus, but it took Leonardo four years before the rest of the picture was finished, except for the figure of Judas. Leonardo scoured the darkest places of Milan for a man with a face evil enough to mirror all the horror of the betrayal—and at last he found him.

It was only after he had painted the man's face into the picture that he realised he was looking again at Pietro Bandinelli. It seems Pietro had gone to Rome to study, but had fallen into bad company. Now he had returned to Milan, penniless, friendless, unscrupulous, and a beggar. So, by cruel irony, the figures of Jesus and Judas in the great painting of the Last Supper are of one and the same man.

The moral is clear. But it is also true that no man sinks so low he cannot be raised up again.

WEDNESDAY—DECEMBER 2.

IF you have striven long and hard,
And yet no heights have scaled ;
If—cruel Fate your enemy—
You've miserably failed,
Still scorn defeat, ignore the pain,
And with a smile strive yet again!

THE FRIENDSHIP BOOK

IN church not so long ago, a minister put a very awkward question to the boys in the congregation. He asked: "Would you boys call yourselves good?"

As you might expect, the lads were silent. They could hardly say they were good, because they knew their parents were listening. But they didn't want to admit they were bad. So they kept on staring at their feet, wishing the service were over.

Then, with a smile, the minister said, "Sorry! I don't want to make you feel awkward. But I'm glad you're honest enough not to pretend you're good; and I want to tell you that God loves even bad boys!"

Put that way it sounds a bit odd; but it's more or less the whole message of the Christian faith. Bad as we are, perverse and foolish, and disappointing and disloyal though we have been, we are still loved and forgiven.

YOU know those electric bulbs that have a frosted appearance—Marvin Pipkin stands behind them.

When he arrived at General Electric as a budding engineer, the old hands there set him the same impossible task they had given generations of newcomers in that field. They told Marvin to find a way of frosting glass bulbs on the inside. An old joke, of course. It would keep him busy while he was getting to know the ropes. They knew only too well that it couldn't be done.

But young Marvin Pipkin *didn't* know it. So he set out to do the impossible, and did it . . . frosting bulbs not only inside but also outside!

THE FRIENDSHIP BOOK

SATURDAY—DECEMBER 5.

THESE lines came to me from Mrs Brown, of
Lugar.
Simple they may be, but how wise and true.
It isn't the look of the garden,
Nor is it the size of the house,
We may be as rich as a monarch,
Or poor as a tiny church mouse,
Our roof may be humble with thatching,
Or noble with turret and dome,
But only the loving hearts in it
Can turn a house into a home.

SUNDAY—DECEMBER 6.

FOR the Lord seeth not as man seeth : for man
looketh on the outward appearance, but the
Lord looketh on the heart.

MONDAY—DECEMBER 7.

MAC'S been in bed with a nasty bout of flu—
not made any easier to bear by a sharp
attack of sciatica.
When I looked in to see him last week I couldn't
stop him talking . . .
" Hear about the American city slicker who
remarked to a farmer that, no doubt, the shower
they had had that afternoon had been good for the
crops ? ' Yes, sir,' the farmer replied. ' An hour of it
did more good in five minutes than a month of it
would have done in a week at any other time.' "
The eyes twinkled. " Just like I say to Alice,"
he added. " There's many a week when an ounce
of tobacco lasts me a fortnight."
I'm always glad when Mac is off sick. He does
me such a lot of good when I go to cheer him !

THE FRIENDSHIP BOOK

BRIAN SCOTT was nineteen, a Dundee lad who lived with his mother and father.

Brian was deaf, and though those who knew him could speak to him on their fingers, he never heard a word, or a song, or a laugh. Yet he was the happiest, kindest lad you could meet in a day's journey.

Then, one Saturday morning, there was an accident at his work. By the time Brian was taken to hospital, it was too late. And on the Tuesday a host of his friends gathered to bid him farewell.

It was a remarkable service, conducted by the chaplain to the deaf, the Rev. John Dickson. Beside Brian's workmates were others who, like him, were deaf. There was a baker, a dustman, a window-cleaner, the man who mends the lamp-posts, a cabinetmaker, and many more. Together they watched in silence while Mr Dickson spelled out on his fingers each prayer, each hymn, and at last, the benediction.

A friend of mine who was there tells me it was a unique experience, made all the more poignant by the fact that so many there heard nothing. Yet their very presence was the finest tribute Brian could have wished for; it was their friendship that had made life all that it was for him.

KEEPING your temper when everything's wrong,
Gallantly, pleasantly, jogging along ;
Doing your job if you like it or not,
Making the most of the little you've got ;
Carrying on when you want to give in—
This you must do if determined to win !

THURSDAY—DECEMBER 10.

IN an eventide home that I know is a gay little body who, at eighty, keeps remarkably young and lively.

On her dressing-table is a small card on which nearly twenty years ago she wrote these words—words she sees every morning and every evening:

I must be sure never to resent growing old—lots of folk are denied the privilege.

FRIDAY—DECEMBER 11.

SOME folk have a wonderful way of making strangers feel at home.

A friend who lives in Canada recalls one of the Canadian Bible Society's most devoted workers, Mrs Arthur Long. She had a genius for making refugees from Europe feel welcome when they arrived in the New World, even if they spoke a language she didn't know.

Perhaps much of her secret was revealed in a single sentence she often quoted: " Always remember, a smile is the same in any language."

SATURDAY—DECEMBER 12.

SOMEWHERE about the turn of the century Bertha Adams Backus was writing poems which have mostly been forgotten—except this one:

Build for yourself a strong-box,
Fashion each part with care ;
When it's as strong as your hand can make it,
Put all your troubles there.
Hide there all thoughts of your failures,
And each bitter cup that you quaff ;
Lock all your heartaches within it,
Then sit on the lid—AND LAUGH !

SUNDAY—DECEMBER 13.

WISDOM is the principal thing ; therefore get wisdom and with all thy getting get understanding.

MONDAY—DECEMBER 14.

HERE is an old story, one which I first saw in an American magazine many, many years ago.

The profound religious faith of Chateauneuf, Keeper of the Seals of Louis XIII, found its first expression when the great man was only nine years of age.

A scoffing, unbelieving nobleman taunted the lad with countless impious questions, challenging him at length, " I will give you an orange if you will tell me where God is."

" My Lord," replied the boy, " I will give you two oranges if you will tell me where He is not."

TUESDAY—DECEMBER 15.

BERYL'S parents gave her a neat red Mini for her birthday—her twenty-first. Only recently, when she had owned the car for a very short time, she led us hurtling along a twisting country road to show us the way as we followed in our own car. The Lady of the House was sitting beside me, clutching her safety-belt and saying what she thought of such fast driving.

That was on the Saturday. On Monday, two days later, Beryl had her first accident. The new Mini was reduced to scrap. Her pretty face was left with a nasty scar which will probably disappear in time.

A disaster ? Perhaps, but also a warning—and Beryl drives so much more carefully now.

WEDNESDAY—DECEMBER 16.

THE postman waves but doesn't stop,
And Gran waves back to him.
Hot tears are shed; she turns her head . . .
No word, no word from Jim.
The only thing she asks of life
Is news of that dear lad,
News of himself, his wife and bairns—
A card would make her glad.
But never a line from thoughtless Jim
To the lonely Gran who worships him !

THURSDAY—DECEMBER 17.

I'M sure that few outside the City of Belfast ever heard of Ted Mullen, yet there cannot be many men more beloved and respected than he was.

Ted was an insurance man and in every house he visited he was welcomed as a friend. If there were problems to be solved. Ted was the man to help. If an old body wasn't sure about her pension or her tax she knew he would soon clear things up. Why, folks' faces lit up when they talked of him.

Then Ted fell ill and died, still in his early forties. So many came to his funeral that his house could not hold them all—so, instead, the service took place outside in the street.

Chairs were brought out for the family and elderly folk. Children from round and about, all of them Ted's friends, sat silently on the kerb. Others from far and near swelled the crowd until the street was thronged.

Together with Pastor Carson in their midst, they remembered Ted, and sang his two favourite hymns. Then Ted was borne through their midst on his last journey. I know it was the kind of farewell he would have wished for.

THE FRIENDSHIP BOOK

MR GEORGE STEPHEN, of Yucaipa, California, is a cheery soul and a born humorist.

One day, he tells me, he met a pal of his who, after a few moments' conversation, said, " George, you're not your smiling self this morning. Cheer up, man, things could be worse."

George goes on to assure me that he took the challenge to heart and really did make a mighty effort to cheer up. " And do you know," he tells me, " my friend was right. Things *were* worse !"

WITH Christmas so near, I am reminded of an incident which took place in our street a couple of years ago.

Nigel, our neighbour's son, was first out of the house on Christmas Day. The rest of them were lying late. He went along to the shop, got what he wanted, and came back to find that he had forgotten his keys. Ring as he pleased, nobody wakened.

So then he went to the telephone booth, to find that he hadn't any small change. " Look, operator," he said, " it's Christmas Day and I have no change. What about giving me a call for free, to waken up the family and let me into the house again."

" Fair enough, and a Merry Christmas !" said the operator, who then rang the family phone loud and clear. " Would you like to come downstairs for your son ?" he asked, when somebody had staggered to the phone. " He's locked out and it's Christmas Day !"

HE that diggeth a pit shall fall into it.

THE FRIENDSHIP BOOK

HERE'S an old story, worth retelling.

A conceited youth visited a wise man who was sitting alone in his library. Said the youth:

"I cannot think how you endure such a life as this, with no people near, and only a lot of books around you. You must be very lonely."

"No," answered the wise man, "you are quite mistaken. I was in good company until you came in."

And the moral attached to the story is:—Good books are far better than foolish men.

SEVERAL years ago, a parcel came to my office.

It contained the most beautiful array of baby clothes I have ever seen. And the letter with them told a thrilling story.

After five years a young couple had been blessed with their first baby, a girl. She was all they had ever wished for. But to her mother, she was specially precious. For the young woman's own mother died when she was a little girl, and she was determined to give her baby all the love and care her mother wasn't spared to give her.

But, at the same time, she thought of young mothers like herself, not so lucky in other ways, for whom a new baby must mean a struggle and sacrifice.

So she parcelled up some of her baby's clothes and sent them to me as a thank-offering, asking me to pass them on to such a mother. And bless her, ever since then, once or twice a year another parcel arrives with its message of gratitude.

This, in its humble way, is my message of gratitude to her.

WEDNESDAY—DECEMBER 23.

*S*HEPHERDS, *simple, lowly, poor,*
  In a stable bowed the knee.
Wise men with their worldly wealth
  Spread their gifts for Him to see.
Grant, O Lord, that humbly we
  Worship in simplicity.

THURSDAY—DECEMBER 24.

MRS AGNES McMAHON is a widow in her seventies.

A couple of years ago, a few days before Christmas, there came a knock at her door. " Mercy," she thought, " who can that be ?" It was only ten o'clock in the morning and as she seldom gets visitors she was puzzled.

What a surprise awaited her ! For, standing in a circle round her step, were no fewer than thirty bairns, all about nine years old, and all smiling up at her. Before she could speak, one of them stepped forward and presented her with a Christmas card, signed by everyone of them. Then another handed her a decorated Christmas tree, with gaily wrapped gifts hanging from its branches. Finally, they all sang Christmas carols, specially for Agnes. When it was all over, one wee lad said, " Cheerio, Granny—we'll see you next year."

It turned out they were in Miss Cowan's class at Craigentinny School. They'd been hoarding their pennies for weeks, so they could give a lonely pensioner a surprise, and they'd chosen Agnes.

Oh, the gifts were lovely, and so were the carols. But what really lives on with Agnes is the thought that the children wanted to share all that Christmas means to them with an old and lonely body like her.

THE FRIENDSHIP BOOK

FRIDAY—DECEMBER 25.

ON Christmas Eve two years ago, a candlelight service was held in St Ninian's Church, Stonehouse.

In the middle of the service, a special offering was taken up for the old folk in Wellhall Eventide Home, Hamilton.

The plate was passed from person to person in the usual way, but when it was brought up to the minister, Dr Gemmell, there in the midst of the half-crowns and shillings lay—a gold wedding ring!

The minister was astonished. Thinking it might have slipped from someone's finger, he announced the discovery to the congregation. But no one came forward to claim the ring. Now Dr Gemmell realised that, just as gold was one of the gifts brought on that first Christmas, so someone had brought a gift of gold to the church that evening.

Who put the gold ring in the plate? No one will ever know, yet I have a feeling that, valuable as the ring may be, the memories it leaves behind are more precious by far.

SATURDAY—DECEMBER 26.

FROM a charming and thought-provoking book by Idries Shah, called *Reflections*, here are two small items which I especially liked :

"I have discovered a marvellous remedy for many forms of deafness : it is called ' praise.' "

"Have you noticed how many people say : ' I wasn't born yesterday,' and act as if they were only born today?"

SUNDAY—DECEMBER 27.

AND the angel said unto them, Fear not : for behold, I bring you good tidings of great joy.

THE FRIENDSHIP BOOK

THESE two stories made me think.

One is of a father and son in U.S.A. They were speeding in father's new car, which he wanted to show off to his six-year-old boy. When they were stopped by a policeman, the driver was very affable, and handed the officer a five-dollar bill with his driving licence. Noting that he was being watched, he purred, " It's O K, son. Everybody does it."

The other story was of a boy of sixteen. His first job after leaving school was in a shop, where the owner explained that when arranging tomatoes for display the ripe ones were put at the top and the not so ripe at the bottom and back of the heap. " Just one of the tricks of the trade," he remarked pleasantly. " Everybody does it."

As I say, these tales made me think. What chance have young folk if older folk fob them off in this way and (let us be frank) show them how to cheat?

THE words were written on December 29, 1928, but they were meant for the New Year still to come. " My Dear Children,

I send you my best wishes for a Happy New Year, that is to say : a year in which you will have pleasure in living every day, without waiting for the days to be gone before finding the charm in them. The older one gets the more one finds the present must be enjoyed ; it is a precious gift, comparable to a state of grace."

The writer was the great Polish-French scientist Marie Curie, who with her husband Pierre, discovered and isolated a new element which they called radium. Like the year now stretching before us, it was to open up untold new possibilities.

THE FRIENDSHIP BOOK

I T'S odd, I know but very true
  That lots of things I've feared
Have loomed like shadows, dark and grim,
  And then have disappeared!

It hasn't always been that way;
  But often when I dread
The breaking of a threat'ning storm
  The sun has shone instead!

Don't cross your bridges long before
  You reach the chasm wide—
It's ten to one you'll smile when once
  You reach the other side!

HAVE you ever wondered why January is called January?

We are about to set foot into another New Year, and it is interesting to know that what is now our first month takes its name from the Roman god, Janus.

Janus presided over the beginning of things. He was invoked whenever anybody began something —a journey, an enterprise, an experiment. He was also the god of doors.

In art, Janus was depicted as having two heads —or, more precisely, one head with two faces. He was thus able to look back and also forward . . . which, after all, is symbolic of what most of us are doing at this very moment. I hope you can look back and thank God, and forward look with faith that all will be well.

From the Lady of the House and myself, a Happy New Year to you all.

Where the Photographs were taken

Printed and Published by D. C. THOMSON & Co., LTD.
12 Fetter Lane, Fleet Street, London, E.C.4.
© D. C. Thomson & Co., Ltd., 1969.